OPPOSING VIEWPOINTS® SERIES

WITHDRAWN

Digital Rights and Privacy

Other Books of Related Interest

Opposing Viewpoints Series
The New Censorship
Teens and Social Media
Whistleblowers

At Issue Series
Mob Rule or the Wisdom of the Crowd?
Politicians on Social Media
Troll Factories: Russia's Web Brigades

Current Controversies Series
Big Tech and Democracy
Cyberterrorism
The Internet of Things

> "Congress shall make no law ... abridging the freedom of speech, or of the press."
>
> *First Amendment to the U.S. Constitution*

The basic foundation of our democracy is the First Amendment guarantee of freedom of expression. The Opposing Viewpoints series is dedicated to the concept of this basic freedom and the idea that it is more important to practice it than to enshrine it.

Digital Rights and Privacy

Liz Sonneborn, Book Editor

Published in 2024 by Greenhaven Publishing, LLC
2544 Clinton Street,
Buffalo NY 14224

Copyright © 2024 by Greenhaven Publishing, LLC

First Edition

All rights reserved. No part of this book may be reproduced in any form without permission in writing from the publisher, except by a reviewer.

Articles in Greenhaven Publishing anthologies are often edited for length to meet page requirements. In addition, original titles of these works are changed to clearly present the main thesis and to explicitly indicate the author's opinion. Every effort is made to ensure that Greenhaven Publishing accurately reflects the original intent of the authors. Every effort has been made to trace the owners of the copyrighted material.

Cover image: Sansoen Saengsakaorat/Shutterstock.com

Library of Congress CataloginginPublication Data

Names: Sonneborn, Liz, editor.
Title: Digital rights and privacy / edited by Liz Sonneborn.
Description: First edition. | New York : Greenhaven Publishing, 2024. | Series: Opposing viewpoints | Includes bibliographic references and index.
Identifiers: ISBN 9781534509535 (pbk.) | ISBN 9781534509542 (library bound)
Subjects: LCSH: Internet--Safety measures--Juvenile literature. | Data protection--Juvenile literature. | Data mining--Juvenile literature. | Privacy, Right of--Juvenile literature. | Computer security--Juvenile literature.
Classification: LCC HQ784.I58 D545 2024 | DDC 005.8--dc23

Manufactured in the United States of America

Website: http://greenhavenpublishing.com

Contents

The Importance of Opposing Viewpoints	11
Introduction	14

Chapter 1: Does Everyone Have the Right to Unlimited Access to Digital Content?

Chapter Preface	18
1. Internet Access Is a Human Right *Merten Reglitz*	20
2. Internet Access Is Not a Human Right *Jon Brodkin*	24
3. Children's and Teenagers' Internet and Social Media Access Should Be Limited *Daria Kuss*	28
4. Young People Need Full Access to the Internet to Thrive in the Modern World *ReachOut Australia*	32
5. Access to Digital Content Should Not Be Restricted by Digital Rights Management Technology *Derek Haines*	37
6. Digital Rights Management and Encryption Protect Information, but There Are Risks *Queensland Government*	46
Periodical and Internet Sources Bibliography	51

Chapter 2: Should the Government or Social Media Platforms Restrict Digital Content?

Chapter Preface	53
1. Governments Should Not Control Internet Access and Content *Margaret Hu*	54

2. Governments Are Right to Censor Some Forms
   of Online Content 59
   Paul Haskell-Dowland

3. First Amendment Protection of Free Speech
   Should Not Apply to Social Media Platforms 64
   Paul Levinson

4. First Amendment Protections Should Be
   Extended to Social Media Platforms 69
   David L. Hudson, Jr.

5. Section 230 Correctly Shields Websites and
   Social Media Platforms from Legal Liability 75
   Chris Lewis

6. Section 230 Allows Tech Giants to Promote
   Harmful Content 82
   Abbey Stemler

7. Internet Freedom Can Promote Both
   Democracy and Authoritarianism 86
   Elizabeth Stoycheff and Erik C. Nisbet

Periodical and Internet Sources Bibliography 92

Chapter 3: Should Individual Data Be Collected by Law Enforcement and Corporations?

Chapter Preface 95

1. Law Enforcement Should Be Able to Use Data
   to Keep Citizens Safe 97
   Palmer Gibbs

2. Technological Surveillance by Law Enforcement
   Can Lead to Questionable Police Conduct 104
   Annika Olson

3. Private Companies Should Not Profit from
   Digital Data They Mine from Customers 110
   Suranga Seneviratne

4. Gang Databases Help Improve Public Safety 115
   David Pyrooz and James Densely

5. Cookies Allow Government Entities and
   Corporations to Monitor Users   120
   Elizabeth Stoycheff

Periodical and Internet Sources Bibliography   124

Chapter 4: How Much of a Right to Privacy Should Internet Users Expect?

Chapter Preface   127

1. Internet Users Need More Rigorous Laws to
   Protect Their Privacy   129
   Anne Toomey McKenna

2. Privacy Concerns Should Not Inhibit the Embrace
   of Useful New Technologies   136
   Orly Lobel and Raju Narisetti

3. Internet Users Have a Right to Anonymity   141
   Harry T. Dyer

4. Anonymity Encourages Abusive and Hateful
   Speech in Digital Environments   145
   Joe Dawson

5. Internet Users Have a "Right to Be Forgotten"   153
   Geeta Pandey

6. Individuals Cannot Expect to Erase All
   Embarrassing Online Information   158
   Keith W. Ross

Periodical and Internet Sources Bibliography   163

For Further Discussion   165
Organizations to Contact   168
Bibliography of Books   172
Index   174

The Importance of Opposing Viewpoints

Perhaps every generation experiences a period in time in which the populace seems especially polarized, starkly divided on the important issues of the day and gravitating toward the far ends of the political spectrum and away from a consensus-facilitating middle ground. The world that today's students are growing up in and that they will soon enter into as active and engaged citizens is deeply fragmented in just this way. Issues relating to terrorism, immigration, women's rights, minority rights, race relations, health care, taxation, wealth and poverty, the environment, policing, military intervention, the proper role of government—in some ways, perennial issues that are freshly and uniquely urgent and vital with each new generation—are currently roiling the world.

If we are to foster a knowledgeable, responsible, active, and engaged citizenry among today's youth, we must provide them with the intellectual, interpretive, and critical-thinking tools and experience necessary to make sense of the world around them and of the all-important debates and arguments that inform it. After all, the outcome of these debates will in large measure determine the future course, prospects, and outcomes of the world and its peoples, particularly its youth. If they are to become successful members of society and productive and informed citizens, students need to learn how to evaluate the strengths and weaknesses of someone else's arguments, how to sift fact from opinion and fallacy, and how to test the relative merits and validity of their own opinions against the known facts and the best possible available information. The landmark series Opposing Viewpoints has been providing students with just such critical-thinking skills and exposure to the debates surrounding society's most urgent contemporary issues for many years, and it continues to serve this essential role with undiminished commitment, care, and rigor.

The key to the series's success in achieving its goal of sharpening students' critical-thinking and analytic skills resides in its title—

Opposing Viewpoints. In every intriguing, compelling, and engaging volume of this series, readers are presented with the widest possible spectrum of distinct viewpoints, expert opinions, and informed argumentation and commentary, supplied by some of today's leading academics, thinkers, analysts, politicians, policy makers, economists, activists, change agents, and advocates. Every opinion and argument anthologized here is presented objectively and accorded respect. There is no editorializing in any introductory text or in the arrangement and order of the pieces. No piece is included as a "straw man," an easy ideological target for cheap point-scoring. As wide and inclusive a range of viewpoints as possible is offered, with no privileging of one particular political ideology or cultural perspective over another. It is left to each individual reader to evaluate the relative merits of each argument—as he or she sees it, and with the use of ever-growing critical-thinking skills—and grapple with his or her own assumptions, beliefs, and perspectives to determine how convincing or successful any given argument is and how the reader's own stance on the issue may be modified or altered in response to it.

This process is facilitated and supported by volume, chapter, and selection introductions that provide readers with the essential context they need to begin engaging with the spotlighted issues, with the debates surrounding them, and with their own perhaps shifting or nascent opinions on them. In addition, guided reading and discussion questions encourage readers to determine the authors' point of view and purpose, interrogate and analyze the various arguments and their rhetoric and structure, evaluate the arguments' strengths and weaknesses, test their claims against available facts and evidence, judge the validity of the reasoning, and bring into clearer, sharper focus the reader's own beliefs and conclusions and how they may differ from or align with those in the collection or those of their classmates.

Research has shown that reading comprehension skills improve dramatically when students are provided with compelling, intriguing, and relevant "discussable" texts. The subject matter of these collections could not be more compelling, intriguing, or urgently relevant to today's students and the world they are poised to inherit. The anthologized articles and the reading and discussion questions that are included with them also provide the basis for stimulating, lively, and passionate classroom debates. Students who are compelled to anticipate objections to their own argument and identify the flaws in those of an opponent read more carefully, think more critically, and steep themselves in relevant context, facts, and information more thoroughly. In short, using discussable text of the kind provided by every single volume in the Opposing Viewpoints series encourages close reading, facilitates reading comprehension, fosters research, strengthens critical thinking, and greatly enlivens and energizes classroom discussion and participation. The entire learning process is deepened, extended, and strengthened.

For all of these reasons, Opposing Viewpoints continues to be exactly the right resource at exactly the right time—when we most need to provide readers with the critical-thinking tools and skills that will not only serve them well in school but also in their careers and their daily lives as decision-making family members, community members, and citizens. This series encourages respectful engagement with and analysis of opposing viewpoints and fosters a resulting increase in the strength and rigor of one's own opinions and stances. As such, it helps make readers "future ready," and that readiness will pay rich dividends for the readers themselves, for the citizenry, for our society, and for the world at large.

Introduction

> "If we the people do not wake up and fight for the protection of our own rights and interests on the internet, we should not be surprised to wake up one day to find that they have been programmed, legislated, and sold away."
>
> -Rebecca MacKinnon,
founding director of
Ranking Digital Rights

In his bestselling book *Being Digital*, Nicholas Negroponte, a professor at the Massachusetts Institute of Technology, wrote in 1995 about why he was hopeful for the future of the internet:

> My optimism comes from the empowering nature of being digital. The access, the mobility, and the ability to effect change are what will make the future so different from the present. The information superhighway may be mostly hype today, but it is an understatement about tomorrow. It will exist beyond people's wildest predictions. As children appropriate a global-information resource, we are bound to find new hope and dignity in places where very little existed before.

When the internet was being introduced to the general public, Negroponte was far from the only technology expert to expound upon the coming glory of the "information superhighway." Many were excited by the myriad of ways they believed the internet would change human existence for the better. These experts marveled that soon much of the world's knowledge would be available to anyone with access to a computer and a modem. They also anticipated the internet would become a worldwide civic forum, where people could share new ideas and perspectives and together overthrow old established ways of thinking about the world. In this imagined egalitarian cyberspace, suddenly the voiceless could find a voice, and the powerless could discover their power.

Initially, there were few calls for the U.S. government to regulate this new powerful tool. After consumers were able to make purchases online, they did become concerned about identity theft, prompting internet retailers to bolster their security apparatus. By the late 1990s, Congress had passed laws restricting the disclosure of digital financial and health care information and preventing companies from collecting personal data from internet users under 13 years of age. But otherwise the U.S. government took a hands-off approach to the burgeoning internet.

The optimism of some tech innovators began to fade in the early 2000s with the advent of what is now called Web 2.0. Increased processing power, storage, and network bandwidth enabled the creation of social media platforms such as Facebook and Twitter, which eventually allowed for interactions among billions of users. With little U.S. government regulation on the information shared and no legal liability by the platforms for user content, these forums became free-for-alls allowing users, often under the cloak of anonymity, to feel unfettered to make statements they would be uncomfortable or embarrassed to say in person. While a boon to the right of free expression, social media platforms also became dens of online harassment, hate speech, predatory stalking, and misinformation.

Web 2.0 also introduced a new business model to the internet, employed by such giants as Google and Facebook, that focused on collecting personal data based on user content and selling that information to the highest bidder. Marketers could now buy personal data on potential customers, often without their consent or knowledge. According to internet scholar Shosanna Zuboff, what she calls "surveillance capitalism" led to "the wholesale destruction of privacy." It also concentrated an enormous amount of power in a handful of technology companies that, unlike governments, do not have to answer to voters. For instance, the First Amendment prevents the federal government from violating freedom of speech, while Facebook, as a private entity, can ban users and censor content however it sees fit.

Governments around the globe have also begun using the internet as a means of mass surveillance of their citizens. For authoritarian governments, the internet is also a tool to suppress free speech, rout out political enemies, and spread misinformation. About three-fourths of all internet users today live in countries that punish citizens for free expression online.

Opposing Viewpoints: Digital Rights and Privacy examines the deep tensions that now exist between the need for people to make use of the internet to lead full personal, political, and professional lives and the loss of rights and liberties that all too often accompanies online activity. The book will present a wide range of opinions focusing on four central questions:

- Does everyone have the right to unlimited access to the digital world?
- Should the government or social media platforms place restrictions on digital content?
- Should law enforcement and businesses be allowed to make use of individuals' digital information?
- How much of a right to privacy should internet users expect?

CHAPTER 1

Does Everyone Have the Right to Unlimited Access to Digital Content?

Chapter Preface

High-speed internet is no longer a luxury—it is necessary for Americans to do their jobs, to participate equally in school, access health care, and to stay connected with family and friends." This declaration appeared at the beginning of a statement issued by the White House on June 26, 2023, announcing a $42 billion grant program designed to ensure affordable internet access is available to every citizen of the United States. Its sentiments are in keeping with long-term demands of internet advocates to improve internet access around the world, seeing it as a basic human right. Many argue that digital equality is now necessary to preserve a variety of freedoms, including the right to free speech and to participate meaningfully in a democracy.

Not everyone believes that governments have an obligation to facilitate universal internet access, often by questioning the framing of such access as a fundamental right. Notable among these detractors is Vinton Cerf, the computer science pioneer who is now often hailed as a "father of the internet." In a 2012 opinion piece in the *New York Times,* Cerf held:

> Technology is an enabler of rights, not a right itself. There is a high bar for something to be considered a human right. Loosely put, it must be among the things we as humans need in order to lead healthy, meaningful lives, like freedom from torture or freedom of conscience. It is a mistake to place any particular technology in this exalted category.

Even among those who do steadfastly believe internet access is a right, some question whether a particular segment of the population should be permitted unlimited and unregulated online access—children and teens. The justification for restricting young people's access to the online landscape are many, including fears of introducing them to obscene or otherwise objectionable content, allowing them to come in contact with predators and other adults that mean them harm, and exposing them to bullying and hate speech that could inflict substantial psychological damage.

However, arguments for restricting the internet use of children and teenagers almost immediately runs into thorny questions about who should be the arbitrator of what they can and cannot see on the internet. Is this the burden and responsibility of parents alone, or should public and private institutions be allowed to censor corners of the internet in the name of protecting young people ill-equipped to deal with what they might find there? There is also an argument that would-be censors are themselves causing harm to young internet users. By restricting the content they must contend with, they are irresponsibly preventing young people from learning the skills and tools they need to make good use of the internet in life and work as adults.

Another point of tension relating to internet access revolves around Digital Rights Management (DRM) technology. DRM allows creators and sellers of digital content to restrict access to the material they produce. Those who support DRM claim it is the only safeguard against widespread piracy, while many digital consumer advocates claim that, while doing little to prevent piracy, it violates consumers' rights by allowing companies to delete purchased content.

The following chapter presents viewpoints offering a variety of perspectives about the importance of universal access to the internet and how and why access to certain online content should or should not be restricted under certain circumstances.

VIEWPOINT 1

> "Internet access is today necessary for leading a minimally decent life, which doesn't just mean survival but rather includes political rights that allow us to influence the rules that shape our lives and hold authorities accountable."

Internet Access Is a Human Right

Merten Reglitz

In this viewpoint, Merten Reglitz argues that internet access should be considered a human right in countries throughout the world. He asserts that today, internet access plays an important role in allowing people to exercise the political rights guaranteed by the UN's Universal Declaration of Human Rights, including the right to express their opinions, freely assemble, and access information. Since internet access should be considered a basic human right, Reglitz argues that it should be provided for free to people who are unable to afford it. Merten Reglitz is a senior lecturer in global ethics at the University of Birmingham in the UK.

"Free broadband: internet access is now a human right, no matter who pays the bills," by Merten Reglitz, The Conversation, November 18, 2019, https://theconversation.com/free-broadband-internet-access-is-now-a-human-right-no-matter-who-pays-the-bills-127267. Licensed under CC BY-ND 4.0 International.

As you read, consider the following questions:

1. What did the UN's non-binding resolution from 2016 say about internet access?
2. In what country do people who can't afford internet access receive it for free, according to this viewpoint?
3. Besides cost, what are other obstacles to universal internet access in developing countries?

The UK Labour Party is promising to provide free broadband internet to every British household by 2030 if it wins the 2019 election. To do this, the party would nationalise the broadband infrastructure business of BT and tax internet giants like Google and Facebook. Whatever you think of this plan, it at least reflects that the internet has become not only an essential utility for conducting daily life, but also crucial for exercising our political rights.

In fact, I recently published research that shows why internet access should be considered a human right and a universal entitlement. And for that reason, it ought to be provided free to those who can't afford it, not just in the UK, but around the world.

Internet access is today necessary for leading a minimally decent life, which doesn't just mean survival but rather includes political rights that allow us to influence the rules that shape our lives and hold authorities accountable. That is why rights such as free speech, free association, and free information are among the central rights included in the UN's Universal Declaration of Human Rights. And, crucially, everyone needs to have roughly equal opportunities to exercise their political rights.

Before the internet, most people in democracies had roughly equal opportunities to exercise their political rights. They could vote, write to newspapers or their political representative, attend public meetings and join organisations.

But when some people gained internet access, their opportunities to exercise political rights became much greater compared to those without the internet. They could publish their views online for potentially millions of people to see, join forces with other people without having to physically attend regular meetings, and obtain a wealth of previously inaccessible political information.

Today, a large proportion of our political debates take place online, so in some ways our political rights can only be exercised via the internet. This means internet access is required for people to have roughly equal opportunities to make use of their political freedoms, and why we should recognise internet access as a human right.

As a human right, internet access should be "free" in two ways. First, it should be unmonitored, uncensored, and uninterrupted—as the UN's General Assembly has demanded in a non-binding resolution in 2016. Second, governments should guarantee a minimally decent infrastructure that is available to all citizens no matter how much money they have. This means funding for internet access should be part of minimum welfare benefits, provided without charge to those who can't afford to pay for it, just like legal counsel. (This is already the case in Germany.)

A Political Goal

In developing countries, digital infrastructure reaching everyone might be too expensive to guarantee immediately. But with the required technology becoming cheaper (more people on the planet have access to a web-capable phone than have access to clean water and a toilet), universal access could first be guaranteed via free Wi-Fi in public places. Supply can start off in a basic way and grow over time.

Still, expensive infrastructure isn't the sole obstacle to universal access in developing nations. The spread of the internet could also be increased by promoting gender equality and literacy and digital skills. Developed nations ought to support these efforts by honouring their commitments to the UN Sustainable Development Goals.

Should everyone in Britain have free broadband in their homes? There are many good reasons to provide the best possible internet access to everyone, such as increasing economic productivity, sharing prosperity more evenly across the country, or promoting opportunities for social engagement and civic participation. And, as such, free broadband for all may be a worthy political goal.

But what is most important is ensuring that everyone has the kind of internet access required for roughly equal opportunities to use their political freedoms. Guaranteed internet access should be considered a human right in our virtual world, whoever ultimately pays the bills.

VIEWPOINT 2

> *"People can and do live without Internet access, and many lead very successful lives."*

Internet Access Is Not a Human Right

Jon Brodkin

In the online magazine Ars Technica, *which covers trends in technology, Jon Bodkin's viewpoint reported on a 2015 war of words between Michael O'Rielly and Tom Wheeler when both served on the Federal Communications Commission (FCC), the federal government agency that regulates communications systems within the United States. In a speech before the Internet Innovation Alliance, O'Rielly conceded the enormous importance of the internet in everyday life. But he also held that internet access could not be considered a "necessity" and therefore did not qualify as something "that humans cannot live without, such as food, shelter, and water." Jon Brodkin is a senior IT reporter for* Ars Technica.

As you read, consider the following questions:

1. As opposed to internet access, what does O'Rielly consider to be basic human rights?
2. What requirements are placed on the FCC to ensure that all Americans have access to the internet?

"Internet access 'not a necessity or human right,' says FCC Republican," by Jon Brodkin, Ars Technica, June 26, 2015. Reprinted by permission.

| 24

3. What measures did FCC chairman Tom Wheeler advocate to make broadband "available to everyone everywhere"?

Federal Communications Commission member Michael O'Rielly yesterday argued that "Internet access is not a necessity or human right" and called this one of the most important "principles for regulators to consider as it relates to the Internet and our broadband economy."

O'Rielly, one of two Republicans on the Democratic-majority commission, outlined his views in a speech before the Internet Innovation Alliance, a coalition of businesses and nonprofits.

O'Rielly described five "governing principles" that regulators should rely on, including his argument that Internet access should not be considered a necessity. Here's what he said:

> It is important to note that Internet access is not a necessity in the day-to-day lives of Americans and doesn't even come close to the threshold to be considered a basic human right. I am not in any way trying to diminish the significance of the Internet in our daily lives. I recognized earlier how important it may be for individuals and society as a whole. But, people do a disservice by overstating its relevancy or stature in people's lives. People can and do live without Internet access, and many lead very successful lives. Instead, the term "necessity" should be reserved to those items that humans cannot live without, such as food, shelter, and water.
>
>   It is even more ludicrous to compare Internet access to a basic human right. In fact, it is quite demeaning to do so in my opinion. Human rights are standards of behavior that are inherent in every human being. They are the core principles underpinning human interaction in society. These include liberty, due process or justice, and freedom of religious beliefs. I find little sympathy with efforts to try to equate Internet access with these higher, fundamental concepts. From a regulator's perspective, it is important to recognize the difference between a necessity or

a human right and goods such as access to the Internet. Avoiding the use of such rhetorical traps is wise.

O'Rielly's other governing principles are that "the Internet cannot be stopped," that we should "understand how the Internet economy works" and "follow the law; don't make it up," and that "the benefits of regulation must outweigh the burdens." O'Rielly was nominated to the commission by President Barack Obama and confirmed by the Senate; the president nominates both Democratic and Republican commissioners, ensuring that the ruling party maintains a 3-2 advantage.

While O'Rielly is certainly correct that one can live without Internet access but not food or water, the FCC is essentially required by Congress to act on the presumption that all Americans should have Internet access. The Telecommunications Act of 1996 requires the FCC to "encourage the deployment on a reasonable and timely basis of advanced telecommunications capability to all Americans" by implementing "price cap regulation, regulatory forbearance, measures that promote competition in the local telecommunications market, or other regulating methods that remove barriers to infrastructure investment."

The FCC is required to determine on a regular basis whether broadband is being extended to all Americans "in a reasonable and timely fashion" and must "take immediate action to accelerate deployment" if it finds this isn't happening. The last time the FCC did this was in January of this year; O'Rielly voted against the FCC's conclusion that broadband isn't being deployed quickly enough and that the definition of broadband should be changed to support higher-bandwidth applications.

O'Rielly and Wheeler have disagreed on several other votes affecting broadband availability and the terms under which it's offered. O'Rielly cast unsuccessful, dissenting votes against Wheeler's plan to reclassify Internet providers as common carriers and impose net neutrality rules, against Wheeler's plan to overturn state laws that protect Internet providers from municipal competition, and against Wheeler's plan to use the LifeLine phone service subsidy program to subsidize broadband for poor people.

FCC Chairman Tom Wheeler said in a speech today that "broadband should be available to everyone everywhere."

The FCC was created in 1934 with the mandate to ensure universal access to telephone service at reasonable prices. Today there is a "Universal Service Fund" to subsidize access to Internet and other communications services but no strict requirement that everyone in the US be offered broadband. Availability varies widely throughout the country, with many rural customers lacking fast, reliable Internet service.

VIEWPOINT 3

> "Support for young internet users needs to come from parents, teachers, governments and the social media industry."

Children's and Teenagers' Internet and Social Media Access Should Be Limited

Daria Kuss

In this viewpoint, Daria Kuss, an expert in cyberpsychology, discusses recent research into the frequency and extent of internet use by young people. After cataloging the possible psychological harm internet and social media exposure pose to children and teens, she proposes remedies designed to limit young people's screen time. In Kuss's view, the problem needs to be dealt with on both a personal and an institutional level. Parents must discuss internet use with their children, while at the same time government and industry have an obligation to educate internet consumers and design products with young people's vulnerabilities in mind. Daria Kuss is an associate professor of psychology and lead of the cyberpsychology research group at Nottingham Trent University in the UK.

As you read, consider the following questions:

1. How prevalent is internet use among children and teens?

"How social media affects children at different ages – and how to protect them," by Daria Kuss, The Conversation, April 1, 2022. https://theconversation.com/how-social-media-affects-children-at-different-ages-and-how-to-protect-them-180374. Licensed under CC-BY-ND 4.0 International.

2. What negative effects of internet use among young people does the author identify?
3. What limits on screen time does the American Academy of Pediatrics suggest for young children?

A report from the UK's communications regulator Ofcom confirms children are avid social media users.

Some 99% of children aged three to 17 used the internet in 2021. YouTube was the most popular platform, with 89% of children using it. Meanwhile, half of kids used TikTok, a popular site which allows users to watch and share short videos.

Most social media platforms require users to be aged 13 or older. Nonetheless, the report found that a majority of children under 13 had their own profile on at least one social media app or site. One-third of parents of children aged five to seven said their child had a profile, which rose to 60% among children aged eight to 11.

Overcoming these age restrictions is clearly not a difficult task. Children simply supply a fake age when setting up their account. Meanwhile, some children have multiple accounts on the same platform—one for their friends, and another for their parents.

The report also found that roughly 16% of three and four-year-olds watch videos on TikTok. This could be children being shown videos by a parent or somebody else, and does not mean they have their own account. But they are still being exposed to social media content at a very young age.

With these findings in mind, it's timely to take a look at what we know about how social media use can affect children across different age groups.

The Good and the Bad

Engaging with social media can have both positive and negative effects on people, especially children. My colleagues and I have shown that social media use is important for emotional support, community building and self-expression among adolescents, but that it can negatively impact mental health and wellbeing as well.

In our work at the Cyberpsychology Research Group at Nottingham Trent University, we have talked to young adolescents, their parents and teachers about perceived challenges and online harms from social media use.

We found that the effects range from spending increasing amounts of time online, behaviour change due to anticipated judgement from peers, and sensory overload, to more serious cognitive and emotional consequences such as attention problems, stress and anxiety.

New research suggests that there appear to be differences across age groups with regards to the effects social media use can have on life satisfaction. In a large UK sample of over 17,000 young people aged ten to 21, researchers found the detrimental effects of high levels of social media use may be especially pronounced at ages 14-15 and 19 for boys, and 11-13 and 19 for girls.

Former Facebook employee Frances Haugen revealed in 2021 that internal Facebook research has repeatedly shown detrimental mental health impacts of Instagram use for young girls.

Separately, we know excessive screen time can be associated with symptoms of stress, anxiety, depression and addiction.

Recommendations from the American Academy of Pediatrics suggest no screen time for children under two, and a maximum of one hour per day for those aged two to five years, focused on high-quality content (for example, content which is educational).

While we don't know exactly what kind of content young children are watching on social media, it's unlikely to be high-quality, and could be harmful.

What Can We Do?

With the recently published online safety bill, the UK government aims to make the UK the safest place in the world to go online. Accordingly, we need to consider the potentially detrimental impacts internet use in general and excessive social media use specifically can have on young people, especially those who are vulnerable.

We need to see increased user protection (such as age verification measures) and harm prevention initiatives (such as school-based education about the benefits and potential harms of social media use).

We also need to see the involvement of community and government organisations in education and awareness campaigns, as well as a focus on increased corporate social responsibility, where the industry takes an active approach in designing products with the best interests of the user in mind.

While we discourage over-pathologising everyday behaviour—for example, we shouldn't assume everyone who spends a few hours online has a problem with their internet use—problematic behaviour needs to be acknowledged and users need to be supported. This can prevent it leading to negative mental health consequences.

Support for young internet users needs to come from parents, teachers, governments and the social media industry. Parents can be encouraged to start an open dialogue with their children, which will build rapport and allow children to open up about their social media use.

VIEWPOINT 4

> "The communities and social interactions young people form online can be invaluable for bolstering and developing young people's self-confidence and social skills."

Young People Need Full Access to the Internet to Thrive in the Modern World

ReachOut Australia

Internet use by children and teens is often depicted as a lonely, isolating, and alienating experience. But this viewpoint published by ReachOut Australia makes the case that internet use, especially engagement on social media, can provide children and teens with valuable intellectual and social skills. Drawing on young people's natural curiosity and thirst for experience, social media can put them in contact with others who share their enthusiasms, introduce them to sources of knowledge, and foster self-confidence as they develop online relationships with a variety of people. ReachOut Australia is a platform that provides online mental health services to young people.

As you read, consider the following questions:

1. How can social media networking increase young people's participation in their community?

"Benefits of internet and social media," ReachOut Australia. Reprinted by permission.

2. How can children and teens use the internet to encourage their creativity?
3. What role can social media play in teaching young people to collaborate with others?

The internet and social media provide young people with a range of benefits, and opportunities to empower themselves in a variety of ways. Young people can maintain social connections and support networks that otherwise wouldn't be possible, and can access more information than ever before. The communities and social interactions young people form online can be invaluable for bolstering and developing young people's self-confidence and social skills.

This will help you to:

- understand some of the benefits of internet and social media
- understand why technology is so attractive to young people
- understand the positive uses of social media and online spaces
- talk to young people about what they use technology for.

The use of social media and networking services such as Facebook, Twitter, Instagram and Snapchat have become an integral part of Australians' daily lives. While many associate social media with a degradation of young people's social networks and communication skills, a literature review published by the Young and Well Cooperative Research Centre found that social networking services actually play a vital role in young people's lives—delivering educational outcomes; facilitating supportive relationships; identity formation; and, promoting a sense of belonging and self-esteem.

In collaboration with young people, we've documented some of the positive benefits of internet and social media for young people.

Young People as Social Participants and Active Citizens

Social networking services can provide an accessible and powerful toolkit for highlighting and acting on issues and causes that affect and interest young people. Social networking services can be used for organising activities, events, or groups to showcase issues and opinions and make a wider audience aware of them. E.g. Coordinating band activities, fundraisers, and creating awareness of various causes.

Young People Developing a Voice and Building Trust

Social networking services can be used to hone debating and discussion skills in a local, national or international context. This helps users develop public ways of presenting themselves. Personal skills are very important in this context: to make, develop and keep friendships, and to be regarded as a trusted connection within a network. Social networking services can provide young people with opportunities to learn how to function successfully in a community, navigating a public social space and developing social norms and skills as participants in peer groups.

Young People as Content Creators, Managers, and Distributors

Social networking services rely on active participation: users take part in activities and discussions on a site, and upload, modify or create content. This supports creativity and can support discussion about ownership of content and data management.

Young people who use social networking services to showcase content—music, film, photography or writing—need to know what permissions they are giving the host service, so that they can make informed decisions about how and what they place on the site.

Users might also want to explore additional licensing options that may be available to them within services—for example Creative

Commons licensing—to allow them to share their work with other people in a range of ways.

Young People as Collaborators and Team Players

Social networking services are designed to support users working, thinking and acting together. They also require listening and compromising skills. Young people may need to ask others for help and advice in using services, or understand how platforms work by observing others, particularly in complex gaming or virtual environments. Once users have developed confidence in a new environment, they will also have gained the experience to help others.

Young People as Explorers and Learners

Social networks encourage discovery. If someone is interested in certain books, bands, recipes or ideas, it's likely that their interest will be catered for by a social networking service or group within a service. If users are looking for something more specific or unusual then they could create their own groups or social networking sites. Social networking services can help young people develop their interests and find other people who share the same interests. They can help introduce young people to new things and ideas, and deepen appreciation of existing interests. They can also help broaden users' horizons by helping them discover how other people live and think in all parts of the world.

Young People Becoming Independent and Building Resilience

Online spaces are social spaces, and social networking services offer similar opportunities to those of offline social spaces: places for young people to be with friends or to explore alone, building independence and developing the skills they need to recognise and manage risk, to learn to judge and evaluate situations, and to deal effectively with a world that can sometimes be dangerous or hostile. However, such skills can't be built in isolation, and are more likely to develop if supported. Going to a social networking service for the first time as a young person alone can be compared to a young person's first solo trip to a city centre, and thus it is important for a young person to know how to stay safe in this new environment.

Young People Developing Key and Real World Skills
Managing an online presence and being able to interact effectively online is becoming an increasingly important skill in the workplace. Being able to quickly adapt to new technologies, services and environments is already regarded as a highly valuable skill by employers, and can facilitate both formal and informal learning. Most services are text based, which encourages literacy skills, including interpretation, evaluation and contextualisation.

VIEWPOINT 5

> "When you buy any media file that is DRM protected, it can be taken away from you at any time."

Access to Digital Content Should Not Be Restricted by Digital Rights Management Technology

Derek Haines

Digital Rights Management (DRM) technology restricts the use of digital content, such as ebooks, music files, and downloaded movies. DRM advocates claim that it protects the copyrights of content creators and prevents widespread piracy of digital media. Derek Haines, however, energetically argues that DRM benefits neither customers nor creators. It instead gives online retailers the power to delete purchased digital content without customers' consent or even knowledge. Focusing on ebooks, he calls for authors to reject DRM protections and instructs consumers to buy only DRM-free ebooks and to create copies of any DRM-protected books they own. Derek Haines is an English teacher and writer who manages the blog Just Publishing Advice.

As you read, consider the following questions:

1. What happened to customers of Microsoft's ebook store when the store closed?

"What Is DRM And Why Is It A Bad Idea When You Buy Ebooks?" by Derek Haines, Just Publishing Advice, August 6, 2022. Reprinted by permission.

2. How can DRM protections be removed from ebooks and other forms of digital media?
3. What does the author mean when he writes "your ebooks are not yours to own"?

Ebooks do not need DRM.
Authors do not need it, and neither do ebook readers.
When you buy a DRM ebook, you never own it.
Worse, it can be taken away from you at any time.

Why DRM Is Bad

A warning signal about the evils of Digital Rights Management (DRM) came as far back as 2009.

Way back then, in a twist of irony, Amazon secretly removed all copies of George Orwell's *1984* from readers' Kindles.

These were copies of *1984* in ebook format that Amazon customers had legally bought and paid for in good faith.

There was no fault on the part of the readers.

It was a copyright-holder issue that Amazon managed to mess up.

If you think DRM is all about copyright law that protects authors, forget it.

It has nothing to do with intellectual property rights or preventing unauthorized copying.

It is all about how retailers control your access to a digital copy of any form of digital media that you buy.

DRM is used for music files such as on the iTunes store as well as for Amazon Kindle for PC, Mac, and Kindle devices.

With DRM, you never buy. You only rent for as long as the provider allows you.

Microsoft Says Thank You and Goodbye to Ebooks

Fast forward to today, and nothing has changed. DRM is still all about the control of digital content sold by online retailers.

In case you missed the news, Microsoft decided to close its ebook store.

But for readers who bought ebooks from Microsoft, there is good news and bad news.

The good news is that they can get a refund on the ebooks they purchased. And the bad news?

The books they bought will be wiped, erased, and disappear from their reading devices and will never be seen again.

This is the sad result of DRM technologies.

If there were no DRM systems working on Microsoft, it could have closed its store.

But readers could have kept their ebooks.

Remember that DRM has nothing to do with copyrighted materials. It is only about copy protection for retailers.

It is not a tragedy for Microsoft customers. They will get their money back.

But the Internet is a vast space for continual change, and so many sites come and go.

Smaller and less well-funded retailers than Microsoft can and have closed up shop overnight.

As a result, buyers can be left both out of pocket and lose their ebooks.

Right so, so long, and thanks for the fish!

Digital Restrictions Don't Work

Are you an author and publishing a Kindle book?

Don't think that Amazon's protected media with DRM on your book will help you.

Anyone with half an ounce of technical ability can find DRM removal tools such as a DRM removal plugin for ebook software.

They can then remove DRM from ebooks in 30 seconds for any copyrighted works.

DRM won't protect you from copying or file sharing.

Nor will it limit the number of copies a determined ebook thief can make.

It is not much different from a print book. You have no way to control people who scan and copy your book in pdf.

Don't have any thoughts about retailers trying to protect your work.

It is worth reading about the Digital Millennium Copyright Act (DMCA).

The interesting part is the DMCA's principal innovation in the field of copyright.

It is the exemption from direct and indirect liability of Internet service providers and other intermediaries.

In other words, online ebook retailers are not using DRM to protect the copyright of authors.

There Is No Security for Buyers

You don't buy an ebook; you only rent it.

Your rights to read it are for as long as the retailer allows you to do so. So forget about giving a copy to your grandchildren.

It doesn't matter where you buy or what reading apps you use.

When you buy any media file that is DRM protected, it can be taken away from you at any time.

You might think that your Kindle library will be safe forever. But are you sure?

Nook owners in the UK found out how DRM worked against them.

It happened when Barnes & Noble sold its ebook business to Sainsbury's, a supermarket chain. Many UK Nook owners ended up with worthless devices.

However, six months later, Sainsbury's closed their newly acquired ebook store and told customers to go to Kobo.

In 2014, the Sony Reader store closed down.

Remember that Sony was the company that pioneered ebooks. Sony directed all customers to Kobo.

But now, Kobo has announced that it is ending all support for its Sony ebook customers.

Over the years, many smaller online ebook stores have closed down.

In some cases, it meant the loss of purchased ebooks.

Even without a retailer closing down, your ebooks are not yours to own.

If you own a Kindle, Amazon can remove access to ebooks you have legally purchased.

Your Kindle serial number is linked to your purchases, so it is easy for Amazon to erase all your ebooks.

It reserves the right to do so under its terms and conditions of use.

Ebooks on the Apple iBooks store are DRM protected and are sold on similar terms to Amazon. You don't own the ebooks you buy.

While it might never happen to you, it is important to know that your ebooks are not yours to own.

It is hardly the most reassuring thought for the next time you buy an ebook from a major online retailer.

DRM in the Wild

For authors and readers, there is no value at all in digital protection.

It offers no protection for the author's rights nor for a reader's right to own what they have legally purchased.

It's a monstrous con and a phony excuse by retailers to protect their walled gardens and profit.

When you publish with Amazon KDP, Amazon sets DRM by default. You need to hover to get a short explanation and then change the tick box to remove DRM.

However, Amazon doesn't make it easy for book buyers to know if an ebook has DRM protection or not.

You have to look at the product details and check if lending is possible.

If lending is not enabled, the ebook is DRM protected.

Other platforms are more open. Kobo, in particular, makes it very clear in its product details that it sells DRM-free ebooks.

Smashwords is another retailer that sells books DRM free.

But you need to check its FAQs to find the details. Here is the relevant clause.

> **What is DRM, and do you have it?**
> DRM stands for Digital Rights Management, and it refers to schemes in which a digital book is copy-protected, or limited to reading on only certain devices. Books on Smashwords do not contain DRM. However, these works are still the property of the copyright holder, and most are only licensed for the personal use of the purchaser. At Smashwords, we give the author the freedom to specify their licensing statement (see Smashwords License Statement below, which is the most common version used by our authors).

But this only applies to the Smashwords store and its complying retailers.

If you aggregate an ebook to iBooks, for instance, Apple will apply DRM.

DRM and Its Negative Consequences

Digital media has revolutionized the way we consume music, movies, and other forms of entertainment. With the rise of digital media, however, came the need for Digital Rights Management (DRM) technology, which restricts the use of digital content. Although DRM's intended purpose is to protect the intellectual property of content creators and prevent piracy, it has several negative consequences for both consumers and creatives.

What Is DRM?

DRM is a technology that restricts access to digital content such as books, music, and movies. It is designed to prevent unauthorized distribution of digital content by limiting the number of devices that can access it or by restricting the way it can be used. DRM technologies use encryption and digital keys to control access to digital content.

Why Is DRM Bad?

1. Limited Access: DRM restricts the number of devices that can access digital content, making it challenging for users to enjoy it on their preferred devices. For example, some movies may only be viewable on specific devices or software. This can result in user frustration and lost sales for content creators.
2. DRM and Privacy Concerns: DRM can compromise users' privacy by collecting and sharing their personal information with third-party companies. For example, DRM technology embedded in e-books may collect data on what pages were read, how long a user takes on each page, and transmit this information to the device manufacturer. This can be scary for users who value their privacy.
3. Incompatible Formats: DRM technology can also limit compatibility across various devices and software. For example, an e-book purchased through Kindle may only be read on Kindle devices or applications, preventing users from accessing that content on other devices.
4. Fair use is impeded: DRM is often used as a way to limit fair use of digital content. Fair use allows users to use and share copyrighted material for specific purposes such as research, education, and news reporting. However, DRM restrictions can limit users' ability to do so.
5. Costly for Creatives: DRM can be expensive for content creators to implement and may reduce their audience reach. Additionally, it has been shown that DRM does not necessarily reduce piracy.

Conclusion

DRM technology was designed to protect content creators' intellectual property from piracy, but it has several negative effects on both consumers and creators. It can limit access to digital content, compromise users' privacy, limit compatibility, limit fair use, and be costly for creatives. An alternative solution would be to create better digital content protection methods that do not limit users' experiences or control, while still protecting the intellectual property of content creators.

"5 Compelling Reasons Why DRM Should Be Avoided," by Arizal Emmar, Yellowbanana.cc, May 4, 2023.

What Can You Do?

Are you a self-publishing author? You can try to help your readers by offering your books without DRM on your retailers.

As a safeguard, you should also make sure that you have saved copies of your ebooks in open file formats.

You can do this by using Calibre to convert your manuscript into epub and mobi files.

Saving your ebook to your Calibre library is the best insurance you can have.

Never rely on your retailer's copy, which could be DRM protected.

With your Calibre files, you can offer your ebooks in many ways, including as an ebook download from your website.

Unless you are enrolled in Amazon KDP Select, you are free to distribute your ebooks in any manner you wish.

For ebook buyers, purchasing DRM-free ebooks is the best decision you can make. Kobo and Smashwords are the two best choices.

Have you bought DRM-free ebooks? You can also use Calibre to import them and make a secure backup library of all the books you purchase.

You should never rely on your reading device to preserve your ebook purchases, even for DRM-free ebooks.

Be careful if you use a proprietary device, such as a Kindle or Nook.

You are leaving yourself open to changes that retailers can make to your device and its content.

Play it safe. Create a secure backup of the books you buy to your computer hard drive or your cloud storage.

Summary

For both authors and readers, DRM is not a good idea. There is no benefit for either.

It does not stop ebook pirating and copying, so it offers no protection for author rights.

It does not protect a reader's purchase. In fact, it makes it more vulnerable to loss.

It is a system of control over reading that would make George Orwell roll in his grave.

The ability to arbitrarily remove books from readers is a concept right out of *1984*.

Can you imagine if the same awful process was available to retailers for print books?

Turn your back on DRM, and say no when you publish or buy ebooks.

VIEWPOINT 6

> "Encryption can protect information when storing or transferring records between different network environments or devices."

Digital Rights Management and Encryption Protect Information, but There Are Risks
Queensland Government

In this viewpoint from the Queensland Government in Australia, the author explains what encryption and digital rights management technology (DRM) are and how they can be used to protect information. They indicate that these technologies can be useful if the information is highly confidential or if the goal is protecting intellectual property, but that there are risks involved with using them as well. Features like saving, forwarding, modifying, and printing are often disabled for these files, and records could be automatically disposed of depending on the settings. The Queensland Government is the democratic administrative authority of the Australian state of Queensland.

As you read, consider the following questions:

1. How is digital rights management (DRM) defined in this viewpoint?

"Use Digital Rights Management and Encryption," Queensland Government, May 5, 2021, https://www.forgov.qld.gov.au/information-and-communication-technology/recordkeeping-and-information-management/recordkeeping/store-protect-and-care-for-records/store-protect-and-care-for-digital-records/use-digital-rights-management-and-encryption. Licensed under CC BY 4.0 International.

2. What is the relationship between encryption and digital rights management?
3. According to this viewpoint, what factors should be considered before someone decides to use encryption or DRM technology?

Encryption or digital rights management technology (DRM) can be used to control access to information. This is different from access restrictions placed on records when or after they're captured.

DRM and encryption may be beneficial when information is highly confidential, or if intellectual property is involved, but risks accompany their use. Read on to find out how to manage these risks.

Digital Rights Management

What Is Digital Rights Management?
DRM is usually part of the software or technology used to create information (e.g. using the password protection tool in MS Word to restrict access to a document).

It works by applying rules to information you create, such as:

- who can view, modify, print, copy, forward, and/or save
- when usage/access rights expire
- automatic deletion dates.

DRM restrictions are attached to records and remain attached no matter where you move the information or what you do with it. This differs from restrictions placed on a record once it's in a system, which allow you to move or change the record.

It is difficult to determine if DRM restrictions have been placed on a document as there is no global technical standard. Some programs will tell you depending on the restriction and the file.

Encryption

Encryption can protect information when storing or transferring records between different network environments or devices.

It is not a long-term solution for restricting access to or protecting information due to its level of risk.

You must manage encrypted records to ensure their ongoing readability.

You should document the encryption and decryption of records under appropriate security controls, and carefully manage the required decryption keys and certificates.

Note: Digital rights management controlled information is usually encrypted.

Risks to Records

Certain features of DRM technologies and encryption increase the risks to records.

Expiration Dates

Early disposal of records may occur when the expiration rule conflicts with the relevant retention period.

Auto-Deletion

- Disposal of records may occur without considering their value beyond the prescribed retention period. Setting up an automatic deletion may mean records still required for business or legal purposes are inadvertently lost.
- Some eDRMS won't allow records controlled by DRM to be deleted.
- Required information and metadata about the destruction of records may not be captured.

Print Disabling

Some DRMs restrict or disable printing, which can affect how you keep records (e.g. if you have to keep it as a paper record).

Prohibition of Saving/Forwarding

- You may be unable to capture and keep a record if forwarding or saving is restricted.
- Some eDRMS won't allow you to capture records controlled by DRM, or restrict actions like deleting or accessing.

Prohibition of Viewing

Records need to be accessible not just to the agency that created them, but also to other agencies, organisations and people (e.g. the audit office, RTI requests, legal proceedings). If access has been restricted using DRM, you may not be able to access or provide access to the required information.

Prohibition of Copying/Modifying/Saving

Records may become inaccessible, unreadable or lost if the encryption and decryption process is not appropriately managed, or if the keys and certificates required to decrypt the information are lost.

Remote Attestation

- Remote attestation means that each time protected information is accessed, there is communication between the DRM system and external servers. Personal data is at risk of being collected by the external server, and that information may not be stored securely or appropriately managed. The collection and use of information must be consistent with the Queensland Government privacy requirements, and explicitly supported through contractual agreements.
- Access can be compromised if the DRM technology needs to communicate with an external server to verify access restrictions or rules. This connection to an external server may also affect how and when you can access the record and how you can use it.

Use DRM and Encryption

Before using encryption or DRM technology, you should:

- assess the need to encrypt records or use DRM technologies based on records' security classification and type, and the business requirements;
- look at how the record may need to be used now and in the future, including access, preservation, right to information requests, auditing, legal purposes;
- think about alternative methods—this depends on how much the record is used, how long you need to keep it and the available safeguards (e.g. restricted access privileges, auditable events history checks, activity logs and network firewalls).

Periodical and Internet Sources Bibliography

The following articles have been selected to supplement the diverse views presented in this chapter.

"It May Be Time to Reinforce Universal Access to the Internet as a Human Right, Not Just a Privilege, High Commissioner Tells Human Rights Council," United Nations, March 10, 2023. https://www.ohchr.org/en/news/2023/03/it-may-be-time-reinforce-universal-access-internet-human-right-not-just-privilege-high.

Brooke Auxier, Monica Anderson, Andrew Perrin, and Erica Turner, "Parenting Children in the Age of Screens," Pew Research Center, July 28, 2020. https://www.pewresearch.org/internet/2020/07/28/parenting-children-in-the-age-of-screens.

Patrick T. Brown, "Opinion: The One Critical Step Congress Could Take to Protect Kids Online," CNN, February 26, 2023. https://www.cnn.com/2023/02/25/opinions/kids-online-safety-act-congress-brown/index.html.

Cory Doctorow, "DRM Broke Its Promise," *Locus,* September 2, 2019. https://locusmag.com/2019/09/cory-doctorow-drm-broke-its-promise.

Molly Hamm, "Digital Rights Management (DRM) Explained," Mass Technology Leadership Council, May 9. 2022. https://www.masstlc.org/digital-rights-management-drm-explained.

Kavish Harjai and Seung Min Kim, "High-Speed Internet Is a Necessity, President Biden Says, Pledging All US Will Have Access by 2030," Associated Press, June 26, 2023. https://apnews.com/article/biden-internet-broadband-bead-0b95fabd7f6833ce420c80d474a145a5.

Kim Key, "6 Ways to Manage Your Teen's Privacy and Safety Online," *PC,* September 15, 2023. https://www.pcmag.com/how-to/how-to-manage-your-teens-privacy-and-safety-online.

Gugulethu Mhlungu, "Why Internet Access Needs to Be Considered a Basic Human Right," Global Citizen, July 14, 2022. https://www.globalcitizen.org/en/content/internet-access-basic-human-right.

Nik Popli, "Gina Raimondo on How the Biden Administration Wants to Get Internet to Every American," *Time,* June 26, 2023. https://time.com/6290366/gina-raimondo-internet-access-us-interview.

OPPOSING VIEWPOINTS® SERIES

CHAPTER 2

Should the Government or Social Media Platforms Restrict Digital Content?

Chapter Preface

Internet technology has been an enormous boon to activists worldwide. Posting on social media and websites, they can bring attention to the cause, raise funds, and organize actions and protests more quickly and easily than ever before in human history. At the same time, authoritarian leaders have learned how to use the internet to find and punish citizens who challenge their regimes. The internet is also a powerful tool for authoritarians to spread misinformation and to censor critics of their rule. Because of the power of the internet to abet authoritarianism, many oppose any government control over its content.

Social media platforms have also been able to seize the power of the internet and use it to their advantage. Unlike the U.S. government, which must respect the rights of citizens set out in the Constitution, these companies are not subject to the free speech protections of the First Amendment. This allows them to censor content and ban internet users at their discretion. As social media has become the new public square, this ability gives them an outsized power in determining whose speech is amplified and whose is eliminated in the greater discourse.

The increasing control of social media platforms over American society is furthered by Section 230, a federal statute that ensures these companies cannot be legally liable for any user content they publish. Often called the twenty-six words that created the internet, Section 230 has allowed for spirited public debate on social media, but it has also protected platforms from any responsibility for hateful and violent content they disseminate. In the eyes of some tech activists, revisiting and revising Section 230 is long overdue.

This chapter presents a variety of viewpoints that take up questions dealing with government and corporate control of online media and explores the pros and cons of their restrictions of internet content.

VIEWPOINT 1

> "The deployment of a 'kill switch' to temporarily shut down the internet on a national scale renewed questions of how to curb the global threat of digital authoritarianism."

Governments Should Not Control Internet Access and Content

Margaret Hu

In this viewpoint, Margaret Hu uses the Kazakh government's shutdown of the internet in January 2022 as a case study in how governments use control over the internet to assert authoritarian power. However, Kazakhstan is far from the only country where this occurs, and in recent years a "kill switch" to shut down the internet has been used as an attempt to stop citizen protests and exert control over citizens in various countries. Blocking internet access hampers political free speech and communication with the rest of the world, allowing the government to have total control over the information people receive. Margaret Hu is a professor of law and international affairs at Penn State University.

"Kazakhstan's internet shutdown is the latest episode in an ominous trend: digital authoritarianism," by Margaret Hu, The Conversation, January 24, 2022, https://theconversation.com/kazakhstans-internet-shutdown-is-the-latest-episode-in-an-ominous-trend-digital-authoritarianism-174651. Licensed under CC BY-ND 4.0 International.

Should the Government or Social Media Platforms Restrict Digital Content?

As you read, consider the following questions:

1. According to this viewpoint, what other countries in addition to Kazakhstan have used an internet kill switch?
2. According to Hu, what is the connection between the increased use of kill switches and threats to democracy?
3. What are Deep Packet Inspection (DPI) tools?

The Kazakhstan government shut off the internet nationwide on Jan. 5, 2022, in response to widespread civil unrest in the country. The unrest started on Jan. 2, after the government lifted the price cap on liquid natural gas, which Kazakhs use to fuel their cars. The Kazakhstan town of Zhanaozen, an oil and gas hub, erupted with a protest against sharply rising fuel prices.

Immediately, there were reports of internet dark zones. As the demonstrations grew, so did the internet service disruptions. Mass internet shutdowns and mobile blocking were reported on Jan. 4, with only intermittent connectivity. By Jan. 5, approximately 95% of internet users were reportedly blocked.

The outage was decried as a human rights violation intended to suppress political dissent. The deployment of a "kill switch" to temporarily shut down the internet on a national scale renewed questions of how to curb the global threat of digital authoritarianism.

As a researcher who studies national security, cybersurveillance and civil rights, I have observed how information technology has been increasingly weaponized against civilian populations, including by cutting off the essential service of internet access. It's part of an ominous trend of governments taking control of internet access and content to assert authoritarian control over what citizens see and hear.

A Growing Problem

Governments using a kill switch to block internet access on a provincial or national scale is increasing. In recent years, it has occurred as a form of social control and in response to citizen protests in multiple countries, including Burkina Faso, Cuba, Iran, Sudan, Egypt, China and Uganda. The number of internet shutdowns is on the rise, from 56 times in 2016 to over 80 times in 2017 and at least 155 blackouts documented in 29 countries in 2020.

The correlation between the growing use of the kill switch and growing threats to democracy globally is not a coincidence. The impact of this trend on freedom and self-determination is critical to understand as authoritarian governments become more sophisticated at controlling information flows, including spreading disinformation and misinformation.

Legal Shutdown

Kazakhstan's internet is largely state-run through Kazakhtelecom, formerly a state monopoly. Foreign investment and external ownership of telecommunication companies in Kazakhstan are limited. The Kazakh government has the legal power to impose internet censorship and control through both content restrictions and shutdowns; for example, in response to riots or terrorism.

Under Kazakh law, the government is empowered to "temporarily suspend the operation of networks and (or) communication facilities" when the government deems internet communication to be "damaging" to the interests of an "individual, society and the state."

Citing terrorist threats, Kazakhstan President Kassym-Jomart Tokayev paralyzed mobile and wireless services for almost a week and invited Russian troops into the country to help with "stabilization" in the wake of the protests.

The Off Switch

Kazakh authorities first attempted to block access through Deep Packet Inspection (DPI) tools to block internet communications, according to a report in *Forbes*' Russian edition. DPI examines the content of data packets sent through the internet. While it's useful for monitoring networks and filtering out malware, DPI tools have also been used by countries like China and Iran to censor webpages or block them entirely.

DPI technology is not an impermeable barrier, though, and can be circumvented by encrypting traffic or using virtual private networks (VPNs), which are encrypted data connections that allow users to shield their communications. When the DPI systems were inadequate for a countrywide block, the authorities resorted to manually shutting off access, though precisely how is unclear.

One possibility is that authorities rerouted DNS traffic, which is how domain names lead people to the right websites, or worked in collaboration with internet operators to block transmissions. Another possibility is that the National Security Committee of the Republic of Kazakhstan has the capacity by itself to block access.

Digital Life Interrupted

The effects of the internet shutdown were immediately felt by the population. Political speech and communication with the outside world were restricted, and the ability of protesters and demonstrators to assemble was constrained.

The internet shutdown also hampered daily life for Kazakhs. The nation is highly integrated into the digital economy, from grocery purchases to school registrations, and the internet outage blocked access to essential services.

In the past, Kazakhstan's government has used localized internet shutdowns to target isolated protests, or blocked specific websites to control information and limit the cohesiveness of protesters. In the early days of the January 2022 protest, some in Kazakhstan tried to circumvent internet restrictions by using VPNs. But VPNs were unavailable when the government disabled internet access entirely in areas.

Concentrated Power, Central Control

The power of the Kazakhstan government to institute such a widespread shutdown may be evidence of greater control of the centralized ISP than other nations, or possibly an advance to more sophisticated forms of telecommunication control. Either way, the shutdown of entire networks for a near-total nationwide internet blackout is a continuation of authoritarian control over information and media.

Shutting off access to the internet for an entire population is a kind of digital totalitarianism. When the internet was turned off, the Kazakhstan government was able to silence speech and become the sole source of broadcast news in a turbulent time. Centralized state control over such a broad network enables greatly expanded surveillance and control of information, a powerful tool to control the populace.

As people have become savvier internet users, as Kazakhstan demonstrates, governments have also become more experienced at controlling internet access, use and content. The rise of digital authoritarianism means that internet shutdowns are likely to be on the rise as well.

VIEWPOINT 2

> "While age verification is not a silver bullet, it can create a significant barrier to prevent young people—and particularly young children—from exposure to harmful online content."

Governments Are Right to Censor Some Forms of Online Content

Paul Haskell-Dowland

In this viewpoint, Paul Haskell-Dowland examines Australia's recent efforts to shield young people from websites that promote gambling and pornography. For Haskell-Dowland, the need to protect vulnerable children from these sites is more important than any concerns over government control of the open internet. Citing failed efforts in the United Kingdom, he does, however, question how effective such measures can be given the technical hurdles to blocking children's internet access, particularly the faulty means that now exist for verifying an internet user's age. Paul Haskell-Dowland is a professor of cyber security practice at Edith Cowan University in Perth, Australia.

"Restricting underage access to porn and gambling sites: a good idea, but technically tricky," by Paul Haskell-Dowland, The Conversation, March 10, 2020. https://theconversation.com/restricting-underage-access-to-porn-and-gambling-sites-a-good-idea-but-technically-tricky-133153. Licensed under CC-BY-ND 4.0 International.

Digital Rights and Privacy

As you read, consider the following questions:

1. According to the author, how much internet traffic is related to gambling and pornography?
2. What are the technical obstacles to blocking underage internet users' access to certain websites?
3. How do VPN providers allow internet users to flout their country's laws that limit online access?

Australia should work towards adopting a mandatory age-verification system for gambling and pornography websites, according to a recommendation from the federal parliamentary cross-party committee on social and legal issues.

The recommendation follows the committee's inquiry findings, released last month as a report titled "Protecting the age of innocence." It identified high levels of concern, particularly among parents, about underage access to pornography and gambling sites.

The committee has asked Australia's eSafety Commissioner and Digital Transformation Agency to work towards implementing the system.

But as the UK's recently aborted effort shows, delivering on this idea will mean overcoming a host of technical and logistical hurdles, including identity fraud and the use of virtual private networks (VPNs) or anonymising browsers such as Tor.

Like most developed countries, Australia has long had laws that restrict underage access to adults-only products. Attempting to buy a bottle of beer will quickly prompt a request for proof of age.

But for as long as there have been rules, people have looked for ways to break them. Would-be underage drinkers can attempt to find a fake ID, a retailer willing to ignore the law, or simply an older friend or relative willing to buy some beer for them.

Just like alcohol, access to gambling and pornography have been age-restricted by law for some time. This used to be relatively easy to enforce, when the only way to access such items was through a retail store. But everything changed when these things became available on the internet.

Pornography and gambling represent significant proportions of web searches and traffic. According to one recent estimate, pornography accounts for up to 20% of internet activity.

According to the committee's report, the average age of first exposure to pornography is now between 8 and 10 years: "It's now not a matter of 'if' a child will see pornography but 'when,' and the when is getting younger and younger."

The report also warns that adolescents are increasingly exposed to gambling advertisements: "Adolescents today are increasingly exposed to gambling marketing… alongside increased accessibility and opportunities to gamble with the rise of internet and smart phone access."

In an era where age-limited content is available for free to anyone with a web browser, how do we enforce age restrictions?

Age verification legislation for online pornography has already been tried in the UK, when it introduced the Digital Economy Act 2017. But by 2019 the attempt was abandoned, citing technical and privacy concerns.

No Easy Task

It seems simple in principle but is fraught with difficulty in practice. Given the global scale of these industries, it is almost impossible for the government to even generate a list of applicable websites. Without a definitive list, it will be difficult to block access to sites that do not comply.

The situation is complicated further by the fact that many sites are hosted overseas, meaning they may have to provide different age-verification mechanisms for users in different jurisdictions.

Credit card verification has become the default solution, as there are global platforms to verify credit cards. But while it is possible to verify a card number, there are various ways to obtain such details.

A minor could potentially use a parent's credit card, or even fraudulently obtain their own. Other ID options such as driving licences could potentially be used instead, but this may not be a popular option for legitimate users because of the risks of identity fraud or privacy breaches. This would also pose logistical challenges: imagine a US-hosted pornography site having to verify Australian driving licence details.

Workarounds Already Exist

Even if a technical solution is found, there are already established ways to evade the rules. Consumers are increasingly turning to VPNs to bypass regional restrictions on media content.

A VPN allows a user's internet traffic to appear to originate from another location. Often referred to as "tunnelling", it effectively fools systems or services into thinking you are in another part of the world, by swapping the users' local IP (internet) address with another address. Some VPN providers now explicitly advertise their product as a solution to the regional restrictions of streaming companies like Netflix and Amazon.

It's not hard to imagine that many consumers would turn to VPNs to dodge any verification procedures implemented here in Australia.

Consumers concerned about privacy are also likely to use the Tor browser.

Tor works in a similar way to a VPN. While it still hides the location of the user (potentially looking like they are in another country), Tor also ensures that traffic is bounced between multiple points on the internet to further obscure the user (and thus their age).

The committee has acknowledged this but vowed to press on regardless, arguing: "While age verification is not a silver bullet, it can create a significant barrier to prevent young people—and particularly young children—from exposure to harmful online content. We must not let the perfect be the enemy of the good."

It is still early days, and there is much work for the eSafety Commissioner and the Digital Transformation Agency to do. It is also clear there is both government and public pressure to identify and implement solutions to safeguard children and vulnerable individuals. But unfortunately, human nature will inevitably render any developed solution as more full of holes than a block of Emmental.

It would be easy to say we shouldn't bother, or that parents should take responsibility. The reality is that implementing any solution will protect at least some of the vulnerable population and will form part of a layered approach. With widespread support, targeted education and age-verification, there is, perhaps, the potential for success.

VIEWPOINT 3

> "Twitter and other social media platforms are not the government. Therefore, their actions are not violations of the First Amendment."

First Amendment Protection of Free Speech Should Not Apply to Social Media Platforms

Paul Levinson

Following the January 6 insurrection of 2020, several social media companies banned then-President Donald Trump from using their platforms. Paul Levinson argues that these companies' actions did not violate Trump's Constitutional right to free speech. While bemoaning rulings made by the Supreme Court that limit First Amendment protections, Levinson maintains that, as private entities, social media companies have a right to control who uses their platform, citing that users banned from one platform can find other means of voicing their opinion on the internet. Paul Levinson is a professor of communication and media studies at Fordham University.

As you read, consider the following questions:

1. How has the Supreme Court, in the author's view, weakened the First Amendment?

"I'm a First Amendment scholar – and I think Big Tech should be left alone," by Paul Levinson, The Conversation, January 20, 2021. https://theconversation.com/im-a-first-amendment-scholar-and-i-think-big-tech-should-be-left-alone-153287. Licensed under CC-BY-ND 4.0 International.

| 64

2. How does the author justify a corporation's violation of the "spirit" of the First Amendment?
3. Why is the author concerned about governments instituting controls over social media companies?

Twitter's banning of Trump—an action also taken by other social media platforms, including Facebook, Instagram, YouTube and Snapchat—has opened a fierce debate about freedom of expression and who, if anyone, should control it in the United States.

I've written and taught about this fundamental issue for decades. I'm a staunch proponent of the First Amendment.

Yet I'm perfectly OK with Trump's ban, for reasons legal, philosophical and moral.

The 'Spirit' of the First Amendment

To begin, it's important to point out what kind of freedom of expression the First Amendment and its extension to local government via the Fourteenth Amendment protect. The Supreme Court, through various decisions, has ruled that the government cannot restrict speech, the press and other forms of communications media, whether it's on the internet or in newspapers.

Twitter and other social media platforms are not the government. Therefore, their actions are not violations of the First Amendment.

But if we're champions of freedom of expression, shouldn't we nonetheless be distressed by any restriction on communication, be it via a government agency or a corporation?

I certainly am. I've called nongovernmental suppressions of speech to be violations of "the spirit of the First Amendment."

Every time CBS bleeps a performance of a hip-hop artist on the Grammys, the network is, in my view, engaging in censorship that violates the spirit of the First Amendment. The same is true whenever a private university forbids a peaceful student demonstration.

These forms of censorship may be legal, but the government often lurks behind the actions of these private entities. For example, when the Grammys are involved, the censorship is taking place out of fear of governmental reprisal via the Federal Communications Commission.

When Governmental Suppression Is Sanctioned

So, why, then, am I OK with the fact that Twitter and other social media platforms took down Trump's account? And, while we're at it, why am I fine with Amazon Web Services removing the Trump-friendly social media outlet Parler?

First, a violation of the spirit of the First Amendment is never as serious as a violation of the First Amendment itself.

When the government gets in the way of our right to freely communicate, Americans' only recourse is the U.S. Supreme Court, which all too often has supported the government—wrongly, in my view.

The court's 1919 "clear and present danger" and 1978 "seven dirty words" decisions are among the most egregious examples of such flouting of the First Amendment. The 1919 decision qualified the crystal-clear language of the First Amendment—"Congress shall make no law"—with the vague exception that government could, in fact, ban speech in the face of a "clear and present danger." The 1978 decision defined broadcast language meriting censorship with the even vaguer "indecency."

And a government ban on any kind of communication, ratified by the Supreme Court, applies to any and all activity in the United States—period—until the court overturns the original decision.

In contrast, social media users can take their patronage elsewhere if they don't approve of a decision made by a social media company. Amazon Web Services, though massive, is not the only app host available. Parler may have already found a new home on the far-right hosting service Epik, though Epik disputes this.

The point is that a corporate violation of the spirit of the First Amendment is, in principle, remediable, whereas a government violation of the First Amendment is not—at least not immediately.

Second, the First Amendment, let alone the spirit of the First Amendment, doesn't protect communication that amounts to a conspiracy to commit a crime, and certainly not murder.

I would argue that it's plainly apparent that Trump's communication—whether it was suggesting the injection of disinfectant to counteract COVID-19 or urging his supporters to "fight" to overturn the election—repeatedly endangered human life.

Freedoms Protected by the First Amendment

Your five First Amendment freedoms are freedom of religion, speech, press, assembly, and petition. The First Amendment can be found in the Bill of Rights, which are the first ten amendments to the United States Constitution.

> "Congress shall make no law respecting an establishment of religion, or prohibiting the free exercise thereof; or abridging the freedom of speech, or of the press; or the right of the people peaceably to assemble, and to petition the government for a redress of grievances."
>
> — *First Amendment to the United States*

Your five First Amendment freedoms are:
- **Freedom of religion:** you have the freedom to think about, imagine, or believe in anything you choose.
- **Freedom of speech:** you have the freedom to speak about anything you choose.
- **Freedom of the press:** the press has the freedom to publish anyone's stories, thoughts, or ideas in newspapers, on TV, on the radio, online, and more.
- **Freedom of assembly:** you have the freedom to gather together with other people in peaceful groups.
- **Freedom of petition:** you have the freedom to officially bring your concerns to the government by collecting signatures from other people who agree with you.

"What is the First Amendment?" First Amendment Museum.

Be Careful What You Wish For

Given that Trump was still president—albeit with just a few weeks left in office—when Twitter banned him, that ban was, indeed, a big deal.

Jack Dorsey, co-founder and CEO of Twitter, appreciated both the need and perils of such a ban, tweeting, "This moment in time might call for this dynamic, but over the long term it will be destructive to the noble purpose and ideals of the open internet. A company making a business decision to moderate itself is different from a government removing access, yet can feel much the same."

In other words, a company that violates the spirit of the First Amendment can "feel much the same" to the public as government actually violating the First Amendment.

To be sure, I think it's concerning that a powerful cohort of social media executives can deplatform anyone they want. But the alternative could be far worse.

Back in 1998, many were worried about the seeming monopolistic power of Microsoft. Although the U.S. government won a limited antitrust suit, it declined to pursue further efforts to break up Microsoft. At the time, I argued that problems of corporate predominance tend to take care of themselves and are less powerful than the forces of a free marketplace.

Sure enough, the preeminent position of Microsoft was soon contested and replaced by the resurgence of Apple and the rise of Amazon.

Summoning the U.S. government to counter these social media behemoths is the proverbial slippery slope. Keep in mind that the U.S. government already controls a sprawling security apparatus. It's easy to envision an administration with the ability to regulate social media not wielding that power to protect the freedoms of users but instead using it to insulate themselves from criticism and protect their own power.

We may grouse about the immense power of social media companies. But keeping them free from the far more immense power of the government may be crucial to maintaining our freedom.

VIEWPOINT 4

> "Certain powerful private entities—particularly social networking sites such as Facebook, Twitter, and others—can limit, control, and censor speech as much or more than governmental entities."

First Amendment Protections Should Be Extended to Social Media Platforms

David L. Hudson, Jr.

In this viewpoint, David L. Hudson, Jr. makes the case for expanding First Amendment protections of freedom of speech to internet users, preventing privately owned platforms from deleting, censoring, or otherwise restricting what they can say online. Hudson justifies this sweeping extension of First Amendment rights by explaining that today the majority of communication between people occurs not in person or in public, but online. The author concludes by urging the Supreme Court to re-envision the First Amendment for the internet age. David L. Hudson, Jr. is a Justice Robert H. Jackson Legal Fellow for the Foundation for Individual Rights in Education (FIRE).

As you read, consider the following questions:

1. What does the viewpoint cite as the "two key justifications" for rigorous protection of freedom of expression?

"In the Age of Social Media, Expand the Reach of the First Amendment," by David L. Hudson, Jr., American Bar Association. Reprinted by permission.

2. What is the "state action" doctrine?
3. How does the idea that online networking sites are the modern equivalent of public parks and streets bolster the case for expanding free speech protections to social media platforms?

The First Amendment only limits governmental actors—federal, state, and local—but there are good reasons why this should be changed. Certain powerful private entities—particularly social networking sites such as Facebook, Twitter, and others—can limit, control, and censor speech as much or more than governmental entities. A society that cares for the protection of free expression needs to recognize that the time has come to extend the reach of the First Amendment to cover these powerful, private entities that have ushered in a revolution in terms of communication capabilities.

While this article focuses on social media entities, the public/private distinction and the state action doctrine are important beyond cyberspace. The National Football League's reaction to Colin Kaepernick and other players "taking a knee" during the playing of the National Anthem is a pristine example of private conduct outside the reach of the First Amendment under current doctrine. But the nature of those protests couldn't seem more public and cries out for a re-evaluation of the state action doctrine and the importance of protecting speech.

Speaking of speech, two key justifications for robust protection of the First Amendment right to freedom of expression are the marketplace of ideas and individual self-fulfillment. These justifications don't require governmental presence. Powerful private actors can infringe on free expression rights just as much as public actors.

The first justification, the marketplace of ideas, is a pervasive metaphor in First Amendment law that posits the government should not distort the market and engage in content control. It is better for people to appreciate for themselves different ideas and concepts. It is traced back to John Milton's free speech tract *Areopagitica* (1644): "Let Truth and Falsehood grapple; whoever knew Truth put to the worse in a free and open encounter?"

Individual self-fulfillment, often associated with the liberty theory, posits that people need and crave the ability to express themselves to become fully functioning individuals. Censorship stunts personal growth and individual expansion.

The point here is that when an entity like Facebook engages in censorship, individuals don't get to participate in the marketplace of ideas and are not allowed the liberty to engage in individual self-fulfillment—just like when a governmental entity engages in censorship.

It is true that state action doctrine traditionally limits the application of the First Amendment to private actors. Earlier this year, a federal district court in Texas applied the traditional state action doctrine to dismiss a lawsuit filed by a private individual against Facebook. The court explained that "the First Amendment governs only governmental limitations on speech." (*Nyabwa v. Facebook*, 2018 U.S. Dist. LEXIS 13981, Civil Action No. 2:17-CV-24, *2 (S.D. Tex.) (Jan. 26, 2018).)

After all, for about 140 years, the U.S. Supreme Court has explained that the Constitution and the protections it provides—aside from the Thirteenth Amendment's ban on slavery and involuntary servitude—only limit governmental actors. Thus, traditional legal doctrine provides that private actors are not constrained by the Constitution generally. This is called the "state action" doctrine. It purportedly creates a zone of privacy and protects us from excessive governmental interference.

The Court developed the state action doctrine in the Civil Rights Cases of 1883. This case actually consisted of five consolidated cases in which private businesses egregiously excluded African-American plaintiffs from their privately owned facilities opened to the public (such as movie theaters, inns, amusement parks, and trains) on the basis of race. The plaintiffs contended that such exclusions violated the Equal Protection Clause of the Fourteenth

Amendment. However, the U.S. Supreme Court responded somewhat cavalierly "[i]t is state action of a particular character that is prohibited. Individual invasion of individual rights is not the subject-matter of the amendment." (*Civil Rights Cases*, 109 U.S. 3, 11 (1883).) The Court said that there were no constitutional remedies available to these plaintiffs and that they would need to rely on the common law state protections. Sadly, there were no such state common law protections either.

Only Justice John Marshall Harlan I, the so-called "Great Dissenter" for his solitary dissent in this case, *Plessy v. Ferguson* (1896), and other decisions, recognized that his colleagues were allowing the government a free pass to discriminate against persons of a particular race with regard to the use of public facilities. He wrote that the "discrimination practised by corporations and individuals in the exercise of their public or quasi-public functions is a badge of servitude" that Congress could rectify under its powers under the Thirteenth and Fourteenth Amendments. (*Civil Rights Cases*, 109 U.S. at 43 (1883) (J. Harlan, dissenting).)

But, in 2018, speech takes place online much more so than it does in traditional public forums, such as public parks and streets. People communicate on social networking sites, such as Facebook and Twitter, more than in any offline venues. The U.S. Supreme Court recognized this reality last year in *Packingham v. North Carolina* (2017): "While in the past there may have been difficulty in identifying the most important places (in a spatial sense) for the exchange of views, today the answer is clear. It is cyberspace—the 'vast democratic forums of the Internet' in general, and social media in particular." (*Packingham v. North Carolina*, 137 S.Ct. 1730, 1735 (2017).)

In his opinion for the Court, Justice Anthony Kennedy elaborated that the expansion of social media has contributed to a "revolution of historic proportions." Id. at 1736. In other words, social media networking sites have become the modern-day equivalent of traditional public forums like public parks and public streets.

This societal development and change in communications capacities require that the antiquated state action doctrine be modified lest the law become ossified. The time has come to recognize that the reach of the First Amendment be expanded.

This is not a novel thesis. Many others have advocated for this approach. Many legal scholars have recognized that when a private actor has control over online communications and online forums, these private actors are analogous to a governmental actor. For example, legal commentator Benjamin F. Jackson cogently explained in a 2014 law review article that "[P]ublic communications by users of social network websites deserve First Amendment protection because they simultaneously invoke three of the interests protected by the First Amendment: freedom of speech, freedom of the press, and freedom of association." (Benjamin F. Jackson, *Censorship and Freedom of Expression in the Age of Facebook*, 44 N.M. L. Rev. 121, 134 (2014).)

Decades earlier, the brilliant legal scholar Erwin Chemerinsky argued that the state action doctrine should be revisited and abandoned. He wrote that private censorship can be as harmful as governmental censorship. As applied to freedom of speech, he posited:

> Freedom of speech is defended both instrumentally—it helps people make better decisions—and intrinsically—individuals benefit from being able to express their views. The consensus is that the activity of expression is vital and must be protected. Any infringement of freedom of speech, be it by public or private entities, sacrifices these values. In other words, the consensus is not just that the government should not punish expression; rather, it is that speech is valuable and, therefore, any unjustified violation is impermissible. If employers can fire employees and landlords can evict tenants because of their speech, then speech will be chilled and expression lost. Instrumentally, the "marketplace of ideas" is constricted while, intrinsically, individuals are denied the ability to express themselves. Therefore, courts should uphold the social consensus by stopping all impermissible infringements of speech, not just those

resulting from state action. (Erwin Chemerinsky, *Rethinking State Action*, 80 N.W. U. L. Rev. 503, 533–34 (1985).)

Already, some state high courts interpret free expression provisions in state constitutions to provide protection to individuals involving private actors. For example, a few states apply their free expression protections at privately owned shopping malls. The New Jersey Supreme Court has applied the free expression provision of its state constitution to allow individuals to challenge restrictive bylaw provisions of private homeowner associations. The state high court wrote: "In New Jersey, an individual's affirmative right to speak freely is protected not only from abridgement by government, but also from unreasonably restrictive and oppressive conduct by private entities in certain situations." (*Mazdabrook Commons Homeowners Association v. Khan*, 210 N.J. 482, 493 (2012).)

The U.S. Supreme Court should follow these examples from state supreme courts to relax the state action doctrine. The Court should interpret the First Amendment to limit the "unreasonably restrictive and oppressive conduct" by certain powerful, private entities—such as social media entities—that flagrantly censor freedom of expression.

Viewpoint 5

> "No provider or user of an interactive computer service shall be treated as the publisher or speaker of any information provided by another information content provider."

Section 230 Correctly Shields Websites and Social Media Platforms from Legal Liability

Chris Lewis

Public Knowledge, an organization that promotes an open internet and online freedom of speech, published this viewpoint on its website in 2021. The organization supports Section 230, a statute that shields websites and social media platforms from legal liability for any content provided by internet users. The viewpoint outlines suggested reforms to Section 230, both for good and for ill in the opinion of the author. It also discusses possible guidelines for content moderation that could help curb harmful and hateful user content without undue curtailing of users' freedom of expression online. Chris Lewis is President and CEO of Public Knowledge.

As you read, consider the following questions:

1. How does Section 230 protect websites and social media platforms from lawsuits?
2. What reforms have been proposed for Section 230?

"Principles to Protect Free Expression on the Internet Principles," by Chris Lewis, Public Knowledge, February 11, 2021. Reprinted by permission. publicknowledge.org.

3. What political and social movements have benefitted from Section 230's protections of online freedom of expression?

Section 230 of the Communications Act has been dubbed the "twenty six words" that created the interactive free expression of the internet:

> No provider or user of an interactive computer service shall be treated as the publisher or speaker of any information provided by another information content provider.

Yet in the past year or so, we have read and analyzed (and written ourselves) words and *words* and WORDS about Section 230 of the Communications Act of 1934, 47 U.S.C. § 230 (which, yes, is more than *just* those 26 words). This simple piece of legislation provides immunity from *liability* as a speaker or publisher for providers and users of an "interactive computer service" who host and moderate information provided by third-party users. It applies to major platforms like Twitter and YouTube, newspapers with comment sections, business review sites like Yelp, and every other online service or website that accepts material from users.

It's important to note, given the widespread misunderstandings and misrepresentations of the law, that whether or not a platform or website is *acting* as a publisher—that is, taking an active role in moderating and selecting what material users see, including taking down user posts—has no bearing on whether Section 230 applies. If you want, you can go ahead and say that Facebook is the "publisher" of everything found on Facebook—the law merely says that it can't be sued over this material for things like defamation. A newspaper is potentially liable for everything it publishes, and a broadcaster is for everything it airs. But some sites accept so much user material that vetting all of it beforehand to the degree necessary to eliminate liability is likely impossible. As of 2019, for instance, it was reported that 500 hours of video are uploaded to YouTube…per minute. By contrast, Fox News, currently being sued for defamation by voting machine company Smartmatic, merely airs 24 hours of content per day.

Section 230 also shields platforms and websites from lawsuits over their good faith moderation practices—even for claims that do not seek to hold a platform liable as a "publisher" or "speaker." This law has taken on an outsize role in the public dialogue about the role of digital technology and Big Tech, as much as for what it does, as for what people think (or merely claim) it does.

There were, at last count, 23 recent legislative proposals to reform Section 230, many of them fundamentally at cross purposes. Republicans claim censorship and bias against conservatives and want less content moderation by platforms; Democrats seek protection for the voices of marginalized communities and from the harms of disinformation and want more content moderation. The vast majority of these proposals, in our view, have unacceptable unintended consequences, either to the innovation and benefits of the internet as we know it, or to our ability to freely express ourselves online. We have a particular passion about the latter.

Content moderation is not neutral. By definition, moderating content requires you to choose what is allowed and what is not allowed. As with mainstream broadcast and legacy media, social media platform companies decide what is allowed to be posted on their sites and users decide what content they do or don't consume on these platforms. By and large, the government does not decide who can or cannot speak on those platforms, in accordance with the First Amendment. The difference with social media, as compared to legacy and broadcast media, is that social media is interactive and boasts limitless "channels." This structure promotes greater opportunity for free expression by all voices, including the most marginalized ones, and encourages a variety of platform options in the marketplace, enabling a user to choose what platform to interact on.

As some online platforms become dominant through various means and the cost of being excluded from a dominant platform becomes high for a user, the stakes for content moderation are raised. It is fair to demand due process, transparency, and consistency of treatment by a platform in its content moderation practices. At the same time, free expression is harmed, not helped, by proposals that seek to limit the content moderation choices of major platforms, because enabling free speech, at times, requires fostering an environment where all voices can be heard, and hateful, abusive, misleading, and other speech does not drive users away. Ultimately, it is the internet as a whole, not any single private platform, that must provide a "forum for a true diversity of political discourse, unique opportunities for cultural development, and myriad avenues for intellectual activity."

One solution to the problem of content moderation must therefore lie in competition policy, and creating the opportunity for diverse platforms to exist, with different policies catering to different audiences. Other solutions can involve user empowerment, not just to switch platforms, but in terms of giving users more control of the content they are exposed to. Regulation and scrutiny of dominant platforms remains essential, of course, and unfortunately we do not have a sector-specific regulator that is focused on controlling for abuses in the digital economy at this point. One example of regulation that could be developed with a digital regulator would be oversight and auditing of algorithms that drive people to specific content. Regulation of platforms must be consistent with free speech principles, both in terms of allowing platforms editorial discretion, and recognizing that moderation and curation serves the broader goal of free expression.

Public Knowledge hopes to advance the dialogue by introducing a set of principles—guardrails, if you will—for lawmakers and others interested in developing or evaluating proposals to alter Section 230. During the last Congress, we saw bills that range from really bad because they could lead to excessive user speech being taken down or harmful content left up, to bills that could create real benefits by injecting greater transparency and supporting marginalized voices through clearer processes. Some of the problems that 230 reform proposals seek to address are really competition-related, privacy-related, or seek to address other problems. These principles are not intended to suggest that policymakers view all of tech and media policy through a Section 230 lens. Rather, as these 230 proposals are likely to keep coming, the principles illustrate the values we apply when evaluating them.

These principles should be considered in the context of Public Knowledge's overall consumer-focused technology policy agenda for internet platform accountability. We develop and advocate for a range of policies that promote competition and protect consumers, including antitrust enforcement, more assertive competition policy, national privacy regulation, greater consumer choice, and approaches to mitigate the harms of disinformation.

Section 230 Principles

1. **Clear Due Process and Transparency:** Users should have a clear idea about what content is or is not allowed on the platform, why their content was taken down, and how to avail themselves of a transparent and equitable appeals process with the platform.
2. **Protecting the Voices of Marginalized Communities:** Members of marginalized communities are often subjected to harassment online, which in many cases means these voices are less likely to engage in the kind of speech that Section 230 was meant to protect in the first place. Any Section 230 reform must consider the effect it could have on these voices.
3. **Streamlined Content Moderation Process:** Content moderation processes should be clear and concise and should not involve an overly legal process for content moderation decisions.
4. **One Size Does Not Fit All:** Outright repeal of Section 230 would exacerbate the very thing we need most to challenge the dominance of the largest platforms—new

market entrants. Policymakers can encourage market entry and promote platform competition by limiting the reforms to 230 to larger platforms or by providing some accommodation for smaller platforms.

5. **Section 230 and Business Activity:** Section 230 does not protect business activities from sensible business regulation, including business activities that stem from user-generated content in some way. Most judges have reached this conclusion already but it is an area to be aware of that may require legislative clarification.

6. **Pay to Play:** Section 230 was designed to protect user speech, not advertising-based business models. Platforms do not need to be shielded by Section 230 for content they have accepted payment to publish.

7. **Conduct, Not Content:** Section 230 has allowed platforms to give voice to so many different political issues and movements, like the Black Lives Matter, Christian Coalition, Arab Spring, and #MeToo movements. Focusing on conduct allows future content to flourish but makes sure that platforms adhere to certain guidelines.

8. **Promote User Choices:** Policymakers can empower users to move to other platform options or create new platform options by requiring interoperability of platforms. This would reduce barriers to data flows, promoting user choice online as well as a user's ability to speak legally on alternative platforms.

9. **Establish That Any Section 230 Reforms Meant To Address Alleged Harms Actually Have the Ability To Do So:** Some reform proposals seek to revoke Section 230 liability protections for platforms without adequately establishing that doing so addresses the very harm lawmakers are trying to prevent. Lawmakers should address the root of the problem and not merely view every problem as a Section 230 problem.

As policymakers discuss Section 230, we hope they will commit to these principles to ensure any proposed reforms do not unnecessarily harm the way the internet has provided a way for more to speak, organize, and be heard in the last 25 years. At Public Knowledge, we will be measuring them against various proposals to help the public assess if any proposals are harming free expression unnecessarily.

VIEWPOINT 6

> *"Just about anything a user posts on a platform's website will not create legal liability for the platform, even if the post is defamatory, dangerous, abhorrent or otherwise unlawful."*

Section 230 Allows Tech Giants to Promote Harmful Content

Abbey Stemler

In this viewpoint, Abbey Stemler explains the circumstances under which Section 230 and the Communications Decency Act were passed into law in 1996. She also explains why Section 230 has a harmful impact on Americans today. Essentially, Stemler argues, Section 230 gives social media companies control over what information and content Americans see, even if that content is unlawful or dangerous. Politicians and individuals on both sides of the political divide take issue with Section 230 because of its role in spreading harmful misinformation and the power big tech companies possess to censor users. Abbey Stemler is an associate professor of business law and ethics at Indiana University.

"What is Section 230? An expert on internet law and regulation explains the legislation that paved the way for Facebook, Google and Twitter," by Abbey Stemler, The Conversation, August 2, 2021, https://theconversation.com/what-is-section-230-an-expert-on-internet-law-and-regulation-explains-the-legislation-that-paved-the-way-for-facebook-google-and-twitter-164993. Licensed under CC BY-ND 4.0 International.

Should the Government or Social Media Platforms Restrict Digital Content?

As you read, consider the following questions:

1. What does Section 230 state?
2. According to this viewpoint, why was Section 230 added to the Communications Decency Act?
3. At the time the Communications Decency Act was passed in 1996, what percent of Americans had internet access?

Almost any article you read about Section 230 reminds you that it contains the most important 26 words in tech and that it is the law that made the modern internet. This is all true, but Section 230 is also the most significant obstacle to stopping misinformation online.

Section 230 is part of the Communications Decency Act, a 1996 law passed while the internet was still embryonic and downright terrifying to some lawmakers for what it could unleash, particularly with regard to pornography.

Section 230 states that internet platforms—dubbed "interactive computer services" in the statute—cannot be treated as publishers or speakers of content provided by their users. This means that just about anything a user posts on a platform's website will not create legal liability for the platform, even if the post is defamatory, dangerous, abhorrent or otherwise unlawful. This includes encouraging terrorism, promoting dangerous medical misinformation and engaging in revenge porn.

Platforms, including today's social media giants Facebook, Twitter and Google, therefore have complete control over what information Americans see.

How Section 230 Came to Be

The Communications Decency Act was the brainchild of Sen. James Exon, Democrat of Nebraska, who wanted to remove and prevent "filth" on the internet. Because of its overreaching nature, much of the law was struck down on First Amendment grounds shortly after the act's passage. Ironically, what remains is the provision that allowed filth and other truly damaging content to metastasize on the internet.

Section 230's inclusion in the CDA was a last-ditch effort by then Rep. Ron Wyden, Democrat of Oregon, and Rep. Chris Cox, Republican of California, to save the nascent internet and its economic potential. They were deeply concerned by a 1995 case that found Prodigy, an online bulletin board operator, liable for a defamatory post by one of its users because Prodigy lightly moderated user content. Wyden and Cox wanted to preempt the court's decision with Section 230. Without it, platforms would face a Hobson's choice: If they did anything to moderate user content, they would be held liable for that content, and if they did nothing, who knew what unchecked horrors would be released.

What Lies Ahead for Social Media Reform

When Section 230 was enacted, less than 8% of Americans had access to the internet, and those who did went online for an average of just 30 minutes a month. The law's anachronistic nature and brevity left it wide open for interpretation. Case by case, courts have used its words to give platforms broad rather than narrow immunity.

As a result, Section 230 is disliked on both sides of the aisle. Democrats argue that Section 230 allows platforms to get away with too much, particularly with regard to misinformation that threatens public health and democracy. Republicans, by contrast, argue that platforms censor user content to Republicans' political disadvantage. Former President Trump even attempted to pressure Congress into repealing Section 230 completely by threatening to veto the unrelated annual defense spending bill.

As criticisms of Section 230 and technology platforms mount, it is possible Congress could reform Section 230 in the near future. Already, Democrats and Republicans have proposed over 20 reforms—from piecemeal changes to complete repeal. However, free speech and innovation advocates are worried that any of the proposed changes could be harmful.

Facebook has suggested changes, and Google similarly advocates for some Section 230 reform. It remains to be seen how much influence the tech giants will be able to exert on the reform process. It also remains to be seen what if any reform can emerge from a sharply divided Congress.

VIEWPOINT 7

> *"Ensuring citizens have access to the internet is not sufficient to ensure democracy and human rights. In fact, internet access may negatively impact democracy if exploited for authoritarian gain."*

Internet Freedom Can Promote Both Democracy and Authoritarianism

Elizabeth Stoycheff and Erik C. Nisbet

In this viewpoint, Elizabeth Stoycheff and Erik C. Nisbet argue that increased internet access on its own is not sufficient for promoting democracy, despite what many people assert. Although the logic behind this perspective is that internet users will use it to learn new political information and engage in political discussions, most users make use of the internet for distraction, such as through streaming videos and music and playing games. People who use the internet for entertainment are more likely to be complacent toward authoritarian regimes. Additionally, these regimes encourage further use of the internet strictly for entertainment by making the internet seem like a scary place that is full of threats. Pro-democracy efforts need to focus their attention on shifting this attitude. Elizabeth Stoycheff is an associate professor of communication at Wayne State University, and Erik C. Nisbet is the Owen L. Coon Endowed Professor of

"Is internet freedom a tool for democracy or authoritarianism?," by Elizabeth Stoycheff and Erik C. Nisbet, The Conversation, July 20, 2016, https://theconversation.com/is-internet-freedom-a-tool-for-democracy-or-authoritarianism-61956. Licensed under CC BY-ND 4.0 International.

Should the Government or Social Media Platforms Restrict Digital Content?

Policy Analysis and Communication and director of the Center for Communication and Public Policy in the School of Communication at Northwestern University.

As you read, consider the following questions:

1. How does the example the authors provide about the role of the internet in a failed coup in Turkey show how the internet can be used to support both democracy and authoritarianism?
2. According to data cited in this viewpoint, what percent of internet users post links on political news?
3. What is a "psychological firewall," as defined in this viewpoint?

The irony of internet freedom was on full display shortly after midnight July 16 [2016] in Turkey when President Erdogan used FaceTime and independent TV news to call for public resistance against the military coup that aimed to depose him.

In response, thousands of citizens took to the streets and aided the government in beating back the coup. The military plotters had taken over state TV. In this digital age they apparently didn't realize television was no longer sufficient to ensure control over the message.

This story may appear like a triumphant example of the internet promoting democracy over authoritarianism.

Not so fast.

In recent years, President Erdogan and his Justice & Development (AKP) Party have become increasingly authoritarian. They have cracked down heavily on internet freedom. President Erdogan even once called social media "the worst menace to society." And, ironically, restoration of these democratic freedoms was one of the stated motivations of the coup initiators.

This duality of the internet, as a tool to promote democracy or authoritarianism, or simultaneously both, is a complex puzzle.

The U.S. has made increasing internet access around the world a foreign policy priority. This policy was supported by both Secretaries of State John Kerry and Hillary Clinton.

The U.S. State Department has allocated tens of millions of dollars to promote internet freedom, primarily in the area of censorship circumvention. And just this month, the United Nations Human Rights Council passed a resolution declaring internet freedom a fundamental human right. The resolution condemns internet shutdowns by national governments, an act that has become increasingly common in a variety of countries across the globe, including Turkey, Brazil, India and Uganda.

On the surface, this policy makes sense. The internet is an intuitive boon for democracy. It provides citizens around the world with greater freedom of expression, opportunities for civil society, education and political participation. And previous research, including our own, has been optimistic about the internet's democratic potential.

However, this optimism is based on the assumption that citizens who gain internet access use it to expose themselves to new information, engage in political discussions, join social media groups that advocate for worthy causes and read news stories that change their outlook on the world.

And some do.

But others watch Netflix. They use the internet to post selfies to an intimate group of friends. They gain access to an infinite stream of music, movies and television shows. They spend hours playing video games.

However, our recent research shows that tuning out from politics and immersing oneself in online spectacle has political consequences for the health of democracy.

The Power of Distraction

Political use of the internet ranks very low globally, compared to other uses. Research has found that just 9 percent of internet users posted links to political news and only 10 percent posted their own thoughts about political or social issues. In contrast, almost three-quarters (72 percent) say they post about movies and music, and over half (54 percent) also say they post about sports online.

This inspired our study, which sought to show how the internet does not necessarily serve as democracy's magical solution. Instead, its democratic potential is highly dependent on how citizens choose to use it.

The study was situated in two nondemocracies, Russia and Ukraine. The two share a common history, geography and culture. Both rank well above the global average of 48 percent of internet penetration. More than 70 percent of Russians and 60 percent of Ukrainians reportedly use the internet.

The results of our study revealed the internet's double-edged sword. Citizens who used the internet for news and political information were more likely to express greater criticism about their country's autocratic political institutions and leaders. As a consequence, they were more likely to demand greater democratic reforms.

But, when used differently, the internet can actually harm democratization efforts. Those who spent more of their online time engaging with entertainment content were more satisfied with living under autocratic conditions. These users were happy with the authoritarian elites who oversaw them and were uninspired by the prospects of greater freedom. In other words, online political use enhanced democratic attitudes, while online entertainment use entrenched authoritarian ones.

And it gets worse.

Tamping Down Political Interest

It seems the world's most shrewd authoritarian leaders have predicted these consequences. They have implemented policies that greatly restrict the internet's political benefits while enabling a rich entertainment culture that carefully sidesteps political issues.

For example, since 2012, Russia has precipitously increased its censorship of political opposition websites and has recently engaged in consultations with Chinese censorship experts to curtail it even further. In China's tightly controlled online environment, even entertainment content is carefully screened for subversive messages. Unsurprisingly, both Russia and China did not support the UNHRC human rights resolution guaranteeing citizens unfettered access to the internet.

However, censoring political content is only part of the authoritarian's "online toolkit." As we have discussed previously at *The Conversation*, authoritarian governments seek to create a "psychological firewall" that paints the internet as a scary world full of political threats. This rationale increases threat perceptions among the public. This, in turn, increases the public's support for online political censorship. These threat perceptions also further motivate audiences to seek "safe" entertainment content rather than "risky" news and information.

When this approach proves unsuccessful, authoritarian regimes instead turn to even more overt scare tactics. Under President Erdogan, the Turkish government has created an aggressive program of legal, political and economic intimidation targeting not only journalists but also average citizens. As a consequence at least one-third of Turkish internet users are afraid to openly discuss politics online. This trend will likely only become worse as the Turkish government carries out its purge of political opponents in the wake of the failed coup.

The final component of the authoritarian toolkit is propaganda and disinformation. Such efforts limit the ability of citizens to separate truth from fiction, demobilize citizens and "undermine the self-organizing potential of society" to pursue democratic change.

The Internet Freedom Advocacy Challenge

Ensuring citizens have access to the internet is not sufficient to ensure democracy and human rights. In fact, internet access may negatively impact democracy if exploited for authoritarian gain.

The U.S. government, NGOs and other democracy advocates have invested a great deal of time and resources toward promoting internet access, fighting overt online censorship and creating circumvention technologies. Yet their success, at best, has been limited.

The reason is twofold. First, authoritarian governments have adapted their own strategies in response. Second, the "if we build it, they will come" philosophy underlying a great deal of internet freedom promotion doesn't take into account basic human psychology in which entertainment choices are preferred over news and attitudes toward the internet determine its use, not the technology itself.

Allies in the internet freedom fight should realize that the locus of the fight has shifted. Greater efforts must be put toward tearing down "psychological firewalls," building demand for internet freedom and influencing citizens to employ the internet's democratic potential.

Doing so ensures that the democratic online toolkit is a match for the authoritarian one.

Periodical and Internet Sources Bibliography

The following articles have been selected to supplement the diverse views presented in this chapter.

"Why Does Social Media Blocking Violate the First Amendment?," ACLU Arizona, September 2019. https://www.acluaz.org/sites/default/files/why_does_social_media_blocking_violate_the_first_amendment.pdf.

Gabe Cherry, "Extremely Aggressive Internet Censorship Spread in the World's Democracies," University of Michigan News, November 17, 2020. https://news.umich.edu/extremely-aggressive-internet-censorship-spreads-in-the-worlds-democracies.

Alex Engler, "The Declaration for the Future of the Internet Is for Wavering Democracies, Not China or Russia," Brookings Institution, May 9, 2022. https://www.brookings.edu/articles/the-declaration-for-the-future-of-the-internet-is-for-wavering-democracies-not-china-and-russia.

Deborah Fisher, "Social Media," Free Speech Center of Middle Tennessee State University, August 12, 2023. https://firstamendment.mtsu.edu/article/social-media.

Mohammad Hemeida, "It's Time We Defend the First Amendment on Social Media," Columbia Undergraduate Law Review, December 24, 2022. https://www.culawreview.org/current-events-2/its-time-we-defend-the-first-amendment-on-social-media-1.

Jason Kelley, "Section 230 Is Good, Actually," Electronic Frontier Foundation, December 3, 2020. https://www.eff.org/deeplinks/2020/12/section-230-good-actually.

Jason Kelley and Sophia Cope, "The Protecting Kids on Social Media Act is a Terrible Alternative to KOSA," Electronic Frontier Foundation, August 29, 2023. https://www.eff.org/deeplinks/2023/08/protecting-kids-social-media-act-terrible-alternative-kosa.

Will Oremus, "Want to Regulate Social Media? The First Amendment May Stand in the Way," *Washington Post,* May 30, 2022. https://www.washingtonpost.com/technology/2022/05/30/first-amendment-social-media-regulation.

Barbara Ortutay, "What You Should Know About Section 230, the Rule That Shaped Today's Internet," PBS News Hour, February 21, 2023. https://www.pbs.org/newshour/politics/what-you-should-know-about-section-230-the-rule-that-shaped-todays-internet.

Steve Randy Waldman, "The 1996 Law That Ruined the Internet," the *Atlantic,* January 3, 2021. https://www.theatlantic.com/ideas/archive/2021/01/trump-fighting-section-230-wrong-reason/617497.

OPPOSING VIEWPOINTS® SERIES

CHAPTER 3

Should Individual Data Be Collected by Law Enforcement and Corporations?

Chapter Preface

Increasingly, internet users are being told they must accept constant surveillance by government entities and corporations. Police departments making liberal use of data collection and facial recognition technology justify these intrusions as necessary to keep citizens safe from criminals and terrorists. Corporations explain that data mining is the price consumers must pay for access to free social media platforms. But for most people, opting out of these platforms is hardly an option considering their now central importance to modern life.

In the United States, where internet regulation is particularly lax, some people choose to simply ignore the increasing erosion of privacy and other personal liberties online. Still, there is a growing unease among Americans about the unasked-for intrusions of tech giants into their personal lives and private affairs. Evidence of this "techlash" can be seen in a 2019 Pew Research poll. It found that, while 71 percent of those polled in 2015 believed that tech companies had a positive impact on society, only 50 percent held this belief just four years later.

The primary pushback to restrictions on data mining comes from tech experts who claim the information companies compile could be used for the public good. If analyzed properly, the vast amount of personal information now in the hands of corporations and government entities has the potential to advance scientific research, medicine, public health, and other areas of knowledge. These advancements could provide enough benefit to humankind to justify the loss of some privacy rights. As mass data collection advocate Orly Lobel wrote in *Time* magazine in 2022:

> Privacy is important when it protects people against harmful surveillance and public disclosure of personal information. But privacy is just one of our democratic society's many values, and prohibiting safe and equitable data collection can conflict with other equally valuable social goals.

Digital Rights and Privacy

 This chapter offers opinions about how police departments use technology, exploring who it serves and who it does not. It also presents viewpoints on whether the loss of privacy due to corporate data mining is worth the possible public good analysis that data might someday provide.

VIEWPOINT 1

> "As with most things, we expect that 21st Century police forces will be able to use data, and extract the maximum value from them, in order to do their jobs. Indeed, law enforcement departments have been trying to do what they can to use data with the goal of reducing crime."

Law Enforcement Should Be Able to Use Data to Keep Citizens Safe

Palmer Gibbs

In this viewpoint, Palmer Gibbs discusses how data is used in policing to help reduce crime. In particular, she focuses on how data is used for predictive policing, which enables police departments to discover "hot spots" where crimes are more likely to occur. The data used includes complaints, arrests, and calls for service, along with past crime data. The goal of predictive policing is to stop a potential crime before it even happens. However, Gibbs acknowledges that there have been mixed results with predictive policing, since the process of collecting data is time-consuming and can be manipulated by officers to show more favorable results. Despite these issues, Gibbs argues that predictive policing can help improve community relations. Palmer Gibbs is the head of information data operations organization for Amazon Alexa.

"'The Benefits of Data in Criminal Justice: Improving Policing," by Palmer Gibbs, Sunlight Foundation, April 29, 2015, https://sunlightfoundation.com/2015/04/29/the-benefits-of-data-in-criminal-justice-improving-policing/. Licensed under CC BY 4.0 International.

Digital Rights and Privacy

As you read, consider the following questions:

1. What is predictive policing?
2. How did the New York City Police Department use predictive policing?
3. How does Gibbs argue predictive policing can improve community relations?

Our OpenData[1] series has been exploring the benefits and challenges of working with individual-level data in the criminal justice context. In previous posts, we've considered the legal, ethical, organizational and technical challenges to providing access to it — even the challenges in simply sharing across agencies of the same government.

And yet the benefits that we know we can achieve through improving access to criminal justice data are significant. In this section of our series, we will survey some meaningful current uses of criminal justice data, some critical national sources of criminal justice data and the next steps that practitioners believe are the most important to take in order to improve the use of data in the criminal justice system to support better public outcomes.

We're beginning with thinking about how data has been used —and is currently used—in the context of policing.

For many people, the primary interaction they have with the criminal justice system is with law enforcement. As with most things, we expect that 21st Century police forces will be able to use data, and extract the maximum value from them, in order to do their jobs. Indeed, law enforcement departments have been trying to do what they can to use data with the goal of reducing crime. While the results so far have been mixed, what is quite clear is that the last decades have witnessed a remarkably broad national trend in police increasingly using data in order to reduce crime.

Using Data for Crime Reduction

One of the most high-profile uses of data in this area has been in the law enforcement approach known as "predictive policing," the use of statistical models to anticipate increased risks of crime, followed by interventions to prevent those crimes from being realized. It's an area that is getting a lot of attention: Last month, the *Miami Herald* reported that the Miami Police Department is working to incorporate a predictive mapping tool called HunchLab, and the Bureau of Justice Assistance provided a $600,000 grant to implement the system. While early experiences of this approach led to high expectations for transformed national crime levels, a recent study conducted with a Louisiana police department (discussed below) found that crime didn't decrease in the test districts that used predictive policing methods.

Modern predictive policing originated as "CompStat," an early data-based policing model developed by the New York City Police Department. CompStat used data to identify geographic "hot spots" where crime would be most likely to occur. It's an approach which drove significant new data collection and organization within the implementing police departments as it relies on having regular, real-time access to data about complaints, arrests, calls for service and crime and disorder data. The collected data must include good geographic information, which is used to map the incidents, and together with additional data CompStat centers make decisions about how to deploy resources in order to most effectively reduce crime.

The broader theory of predictive policing is that physical proof of "community disorder," combined with other data, provides indicators of likely future crimes in an area. In this sense, predictive policing builds on the narrative underlying the "broken windows" theory established in 1982 by social scientists James Q. Wilson and George L. Kelling. The broken windows theory asserts that if a vandalized building is not repaired, more crime is likely to take place in that neighborhood. By fixing up smaller issues, like a building's smashed windows, a sense of order is created in the community and that helps to keep more significant crime at bay. If police departments focus their resources on these areas where crimes are predicted to happen at higher rates, the assumption is that additional police presence will allow them to "deter and preempt crimes."

The predictive policing approach has received both enormous praise and substantial criticism. CompStat achieved such strong early support because it appeared to have led to very large reductions in crime in New York City in its earliest implementation. However, later implementations have had less demonstrable success, an outcome that some analysts have attributed to a mismatch between the data-focused process and the complex organizational aspects of intervention.

In addition, the data-focused approach has produced some unintended consequences that create their own problems. One issue stems from the fact that police data has become such an important internal accountability tool that it encourages a degree of cheating, and police officers have been documented inappropriately manipulating data in order to produce more flattering results.

The rise of controversial stop-and-frisk practices are also associated with the CompStat model, a topic we explored in an earlier post. In response to the widespread observation of unconstitutional and overuse of stop and frisk by the New York Police Department, a series of class action lawsuits were filed against the city.

Predictive Policing Study

Predictive policing is the most current incarnation of the data-based policing approach, and while it has been the subject of both anecdotal support and incident-based criticism, it lacked impartial analysis. For that reason, in 2012, the National Institute of Justice funded a seven-month-long trial study with the Shreveport Police Department that used predictive policing methods. The study was conducted by the RAND Corporation as part of its Safety and Justice Program.

The Shreveport PD had been using a more traditional policing strategy, where officers were deployed to certain areas in response to "hot spots" of crime. But the department wanted to predict the development of these hot spots; it wanted to be able to prevent crime rather than simply react to it.

The department worked off different sets of maps—the control districts used maps with information about recent crime, while the test districts used maps that reflected the statistical predictions. The goal was to reduce property crime (which the department defined as residential burglaries, business burglaries, residential thefts, business thefts, thefts from vehicles and vehicle thefts) and "increase quality arrests" (which was defined as arrests of people who committed one of the six types of property crime or who had a serious criminal history).

In discussing the trial, officers noted that these directives were different from other operations, which usually placed a premium on increasing the overall number of arrests rather than the number of quality arrests.

The officers in the test districts emphasized developing relationships within the neighborhood to aid in intelligence gathering: The objective was to "get actionable information for crime prevention and clearing crimes," with an "emphasis on intelligence gathering through leveraging low-level offenders and offenses."

The officers in the Shreveport Police Department also noted that the data on the predictive maps allowed them to strategize exactly where and when they should focus resources. "Since the maps consisted of fairly small grid squares, officers were able to develop strategies for highly focused, specific areas, which allowed units to be more effective," the study's authors wrote.

Overall, however, the RAND study found that "for the Shreveport predictive policing experiment, there is no statistical evidence that special operations to target property crime informed by predictive maps resulted in greater crime reductions than special operations informed by conventional crime maps."

The study's authors questioned whether or not "a map identifying hot spots based on a predictive model, rather than a traditional map that identifies hot spots based on prior crime locations, is necessary." In fact, the commander in one of the test groups told researchers that "unless predictive products could provide very high levels of accuracy, literally specifying where and when specific crimes were highly likely to occur, the predictions were just providing traditional hot spots, and interventions could only be typical hot spots interventions."

That's an important distinction to make, since the report described the trial as "very time-consuming." The team reported that creating the predictions was "an arduous task" and "the amount of effort was unsustainable in the long term (i.e., more than six months)."

The Shreveport PD reported that it was difficult to recruit officers for the trial, noting that the predictive policing work required extra time because officers had to collect more information than normal (they said they spent at most 30 minutes talking with each "suspicious" individual). The trial also required monthly meetings, where the department's leadership team would receive the predictions and then coordinate action based on that data. This was described as a "key element" of the trial, but the meetings didn't happen. The study's authors wrote:

> It is not clear whether the development of a collective group to decide on intelligence-led activities was not feasible, realistic, or ideal. There are a number of reasons why developing a group to build consensus on activities in two commands for half a year was difficult: commander management styles, ideologies on policing, neighborhood infrastructure design, and so on.

Improved Community Relations

Although the report found that predictive policing is not more effective than traditional policing tools like hot spot maps, officers did report some successes during the trial, the most significant of which was improved relations with community members.

A key piece of the trial was increased communication between officers and suspicious people and criminals—cops asked more follow-up questions after crimes happened. The officers said that after seeing these interactions, people were "more willing" to share information and provide tips with the police department. Officers said that people in the neighborhood waved "hello to patrol cars," which didn't happen before the experiment. The officers told the researchers, "The core value of PILOT was in their command's focused patrols that were collecting better information on criminal activity and building better relations with the community, not in the predictive maps themselves."

Thus, although the intended effect of the predictive policing trial did not increase the department's direct effectiveness over earlier traditional methods, the trial did appear to have other positive effects: improved police-community relations.

VIEWPOINT 2

> "There has been serious backlash from privacy rights groups, the general public, universities, and some members of Congress against racial bias in the use of the technology."

Technological Surveillance by Law Enforcement Can Lead to Questionable Police Conduct

Annika Olson

In this viewpoint, Annika Olson critiques law enforcement's use of technological surveillance, specifically focusing on facial recognition software. Unregulated by the federal government, this software is increasingly employed by urban police departments. Olson argues that it has been employed disproportionately in Black and Brown communities, reflecting a pervasive bias against these populations. She also cites that the software often yields inaccurate results among minority groups, increasing the possibility of false arrests. In 2022, Annika Olson was the Assistant Director of Policy Research for the Institute for Urban Policy Research and Analysis (IUPRA) at University of Texas at Austin.

"Facial Recognition Tech Perpetuates Racial Bias. So Why Are We Still Using It?," by Annika Olson, Yes Media, December 9, 2021. Reprinted by permission.

Should Individual Data Be Collected by Law Enforcement and Corporations?

As you read, consider the following questions:

1. How does law enforcement's use of facial recognition software hurt Black and Brown communities?
2. With which population groups does facial recognition software have the highest failure rate?
3. How many Americans are in law enforcement's facial recognition network?

Most iPhone users unlock their phones with a quick glance. Many of us have Ring video doorbells to see who's outside when there's a knock. We take for granted how Facebook knows every single person to tag in a posted photo.

While this use of facial recognition technology is seemingly convenient—and cool, like something in a science fiction movie—the industry is currently completely unregulated by the federal government.

In this ever-evolving technological world, it is time for both grassroots solutions and federal regulation. Or, at the very least, lawmakers ought to require transparency from the producers of the deeply problematic technology.

How Facial Recognition Fuels Racial Profiling

The most serious danger may be its use by law enforcement and how the lives of Black and Brown communities are subsequently being put at risk. If we don't act swiftly, we may be in for a real-life episode of *Black Mirror*—a sci-fi TV show depicting the consequences of a high-tech future—with communities of color at the center of the dystopia.

Here's why: Black Americans are already more likely than White Americans to be arrested and locked up for minor crimes. As a result, Black people are overrepresented in mug shot data, which is used by facial recognition software to identify suspects accused of committing crimes.

This ultimately creates a feed-forward loop where: 1. racial profiling by police leads to the disproportionate arrest of people of color; 2. facial recognition technology, in turn, uses arrest data (mug shots) borne from discrimination; and 3. that data continues to fuel more racial discrimination via surveillance of communities of color.

In a real-world example of the racist use of the technology, the city of Detroit enacted Project Green Light in 2016, installing cameras with facial recognition software to scoop up data from across the city and stream it directly to the police department. These PGL systems were disproportionately located in majority-Black areas, and reports show that the surveillance is linked to the criminalization of Black and Brown residents and subsequently the loss of public benefits and housing.

How the Technology Is Inherently Racist

Not only is the geographic placement of facial recognition technology by law enforcement blatantly racist; the software itself shows significant bias. A study by the Massachusetts Institute of Technology called "Gender Shades: Intersectional Accuracy Disparities in Commercial Gender Classification" found that the software consistently had the most inaccurate results for people who are female, ages 18–30, and Black. Specifically, the facial recognition software performs worse on darker-skinned women, with error rates of more than 40%, compared with White males. This is true across all platforms—from IBM to Microsoft to Amazon—and was corroborated by the federal government.

Another study by the National Institute of Standards and Technology found that the algorithms work best at recognizing middle-aged White men and don't work as well on children, the elderly, people of color, or women. In fact, error rates tend to be highest for Black women, just as the MIT study found.

SURVEILLANCE AND THE PATRIOT ACT

Hastily passed 45 days after 9/11 in the name of national security, the Patriot Act was the first of many changes to surveillance laws that made it easier for the government to spy on ordinary Americans by expanding the authority to monitor phone and email communications, collect bank and credit reporting records, and track the activity of innocent Americans on the Internet. While most Americans think it was created to catch terrorists, the Patriot Act actually turns regular citizens into suspects.

National Security Letters (NSLs) are issued by FBI agents, without a judge's approval, to obtain personal information.

Abuse of privacy: The Patriot Act does not require information obtained by NSLs to be destroyed—even if the information is determined to concern innocent Americans.

At least 34,00 law enforcement and intelligence agents have access to phone records collected through NSLs.

In response to 9 NSLs, 11,100 Americans' telephone account records were turned over to the FBI.

The Patriot Act prohibits Americans who receive NSLs from telling anyone. These "gag order" provisions have been held unconstitutional in several legal cases.

Between 2003 and 2005, the FBI made 53 reported criminal referrals to prosecutors as a result of 143,074 NSLs.

"Sneak and Peek" Searches: The Patriot Act allows federal law enforcement agencies to delay giving notice when they conduct secret searches of Americans' homes and offices—a fundamental change to Fourth Amendment privacy protections and search warrants. This means that government agents can enter a house, apartment, or office with a search warrant when the occupant is away, search through his/her property and take photographs—in some cases seizing property and electronic communications—and not tell the owner until later.

"Surveillance Under the Patriot Act," American Civil Liberties Union.

The Problematic History of Facial Recognition

The roots of facial recognition technology date back to the 1960s, when Woodrow Wilson Bledsoe began developing a system of measurements to classify photos of faces.

By 2001, law enforcement was using the technology on crowds entering the Super Bowl, comparing the faces of people who walked through the turnstiles to mug shots of known criminals.

In 2014, Facebook unveiled its DeepFace photo-tagging software, and by 2017, Apple introduced its new iPhone X, which utilized the technology as a way for people to unlock their devices. As per the Georgetown Law Center on Privacy and Technology, half of all American adults are in a law enforcement recognition network. So, if you're sitting on a bus next to someone else, chances are one of you is in the system.

Over the past several years, major tech players like Amazon, IBM, and Microsoft have been selling their facial recognition software to law enforcement for mass surveillance. This unregulated and unchecked system has served to enhance discriminatory practices by law enforcement and further endanger the lives of communities of color.

How the Public Is Fighting Back

On the bright side, there has been serious backlash from privacy rights groups, the general public, universities, and some members of Congress against racial bias in the use of the technology. One creative protest consisted of political activists in London wearing asymmetric makeup in patterns that make it impossible for their faces to be matched to a database. The idea was developed by artist Adam Harvey, who coined the term "computer vision dazzle," meaning a modern form of the camouflage used in World War I by the Royal Navy.

Responding to increasing public outrage, in June 2020, IBM, Microsoft, and Amazon said they would not sell their technology to law enforcement agencies for a year. The year is now up, and Amazon has extended its ban until further notice, but the fight is far from over.

Meanwhile, cities like San Francisco, Oakland, Boston, and Portland, Oregon, have gone further than the private sector and outlawed the use of citywide surveillance technology, with more cities and states sure to follow suit.

However, because there are currently no federal laws that regulate facial recognition technology, we are depending on piecemeal legislation in cities and states across the country—a flawed solution to a complicated problem.

If the federal government does not step in and officially ban the technology that is disproportionately impacting the lives of Black and Brown communities, at the very least it must require that big-tech companies be transparent about the stark, racist biases in their algorithms.

If not, the storylines on *Black Mirror* won't be just fictitious.

VIEWPOINT 3

> *"It's almost impossible to know if user data is being misused within company bounds or in business-to-business interaction."*

Private Companies Should Not Profit from Digital Data They Mine from Customers
Suranga Seneviratne

Suranga Seneviratne cites that a majority of the population in his native Australia is concerned about how their digital information is being used by for-profit companies. He recounts recent scandals that revealed certain companies were mining data unbeknownst to their customers, further eroding public trust in any corporation's pledge to not exploit personal digital information and to respect their customers' privacy. Seneviratne lists lawsuits, regulatory fines, and industry whistleblowers as possible tools to combat widespread data mining. Suranga Seneviratne is a senior security lecturer in the School of IT at the University of Sydney in Australia.

As you read, consider the following questions:

1. What was the Cambridge Analytica scandal?
2. Why is it often difficult to opt out of data collection?

"The ugly truth: tech companies are tracking and misusing our data, and there's little we can do," by Suranga Seneviratne, The Conversation, November 26, 2019. https://theconversation.com/the-ugly-truth-tech-companies-are-tracking-and-misusing-our-data-and-theres-little-we-can-do-127444. Licensed under CC-BY-ND 4.0 International.

3. How effective are government regulations in policing companies' undeclared collection of user data?

As survey results pile, it's becoming clear Australians are sceptical about how their online data is tracked and used. But one question worth asking is: are our fears founded?

The short answer is: yes.

In a survey of 2,000 people completed last year, Privacy Australia found 57.9% of participants weren't confident companies would take adequate measures to protect their data.

Similar scepticism was noted in results from the 2017 Australian Community Attitudes to Privacy Survey of 1,800 people, which found:

- 79% of participants felt uncomfortable with targeted advertising based on their online activities
- 83% were uncomfortable with social networking companies keeping their information
- 66% believed it was standard practice for mobile apps to collect user information and
- 74% believed it was standard practice for websites to collect user information.

Also in 2017, the Digital Rights in Australia report, prepared by the University of Sydney's Digital Rights and Governance Project, revealed 62% of 1,600 participants felt they weren't in control of their online privacy. About 47% were also concerned the government could violate their privacy.

The Ugly Truth

Lately, a common pattern has emerged every time malpractice is exposed.

The company involved will provide an "opt-out" mechanism for users, or a dashboard to see what personal data is being collected (for example, Google Privacy Checkup), along with an apology.

If we opt-out, does this mean they stop collecting our data? Would they reveal collected data to us? And if we requested to have our data deleted, would they do so?

To be blunt, we don't know. And as end users there's not much we can do about it, anyway.

When it comes to personal data, it's extremely difficult to identify unlawful collections among legitimate collections, because multiple factors need to be considered, including the context in which the data is collected, the methodology used to obtain user consent, and country-specific laws.

Also, it's almost impossible to know if user data is being misused within company bounds or in business-to-business interactions.

Despite ongoing public outcry to protect online privacy, last year we witnessed the Cambridge Analytica scandal, in which a third party company was able to gather the personal information of millions of Facebook users and use it in political campaigns.

Earlier this year, both Amazon and Apple were reported to be using human annotators to listen to personal conversations, recorded via their respective digital assistants Alexa and Siri.

More recently, a *New York Times* article exposed how much fine granular data is acquired and maintained by relatively unknown consumer scoring companies. In one case, a third-party company knew the writer Kashmir Hill used her iPhone to order chicken tikka masala, vegetable samosas, and garlic naan on a Saturday night in April, three years ago.

At this rate, without any action, scepticism towards online privacy will only increase.

History Is a Teacher

Early this year, we witnessed the bitter end of the Do-Not-Track initiative. This was proposed as a privacy feature where requests made by an internet browser contained a flag, asking remote web servers to not track users. However, there was no legal framework to force web server compliance, so many web servers ended up discarding this flag.

Many companies have made it too difficult to opt-out from data collections, or request the deletion of all data related to an individual.

For example, as a solution to the backlash on human voice command annotation, Apple provided an opt-out mechanism. However, doing this for an Apple device is not straightforward, and the option isn't prominent in the device settings.

Also, it's clear tech companies don't want to have opting-out of tracking as users' default setting.

It's worth noting that since Australia doesn't have social media or internet giants, much of the country's privacy-related debates are focused on government legislation.

Are Regulatory Safeguards Useful?

But there is some hope left. Some recent events have prompted tech companies to think twice about the undeclared collection of user data.

For example, a US$5 billion fine is on air for Facebook, for its role in the Cambridge Analytica incident, and related practices of sharing user data with third parties. The exposure of this event has forced Facebook to take measures to improve its privacy controls and be forthcoming with users.

Similarly Google was fined EU$50 million under the General Data Protection Regulation by French data regulator CNIL, for lack of transparency and consent in user-targeted ads.

Like Facebook, Google responded by taking measures to improve the privacy of users, by stopping reading our e-mails to provide targeted ads, enhancing its privacy control dashboard, and revealing its vision to keep user data in devices rather than in the cloud.

No Time to Be Complacent

While it's clear current regulatory safeguards are having a positive effect on online privacy, there is ongoing debate about whether they are sufficient.

Some have argued about possible loopholes in the European Union's General Data Protection Regulation, and the fact that some definitions of legitimate use of personal data leave room for interpretation.

Tech giants are multiple steps ahead of regulators, and are in a position to exploit any grey areas in legislation they can find.

We can't rely on accidental leaks or whistleblowers to hold them accountable.

Respect for user privacy and ethical usage of personal data must come intrinsically from within these companies themselves.

VIEWPOINT 4

> "These data help the police solve gang-related crimes and flag gang members who might benefit from social services."

Gang Databases Help Improve Public Safety

David Pyrooz and James Densely

In this viewpoint, David Pyrooz and James Densely explain that although gang databases have been on the decline in recent years, they play an important role in law enforcement and public safety. Gang-related homicides are a significant issue in the U.S. and collecting data that helps identify gang members can help solve crimes and prevent them from happening by offering social services to people involved with gangs. The authors assert that changing how data is collected by giving people included in the database the right to know they are in it and to challenge this designation if it's inaccurate could help improve the quality of data and respect individual rights. David Pyrooz is an associate professor of sociology at University of Colorado Boulder, and James Densely is a professor of criminal justice at Metropolitan State University.

As you read, consider the following questions:

1. At the time this viewpoint was published in 2018, how many states had laws on gang databases?

"Is gang activity on the rise? A movement to abolish gang databases makes it hard to tell," by David Pyrooz and James Densely, The Conversation, July 5, 2018, https://theconversation.com/is-gang-activity-on-the-rise-a-movement-to-abolish-gang-databases-makes-it-hard-to-tell-99252. Licensed under CC BY-ND 4.0 International.

2. According to the authors, what has caused there to be less data on gangs?
3. What are the criticisms of gang databases mentioned in this viewpoint? How do the authors address these criticisms?

President Donald Trump has frequently spoken about dangerous gang members from MS-13 "infesting" the United States.

It's important to be able to confirm or debunk those statements. But a movement among criminal justice reformers may make that more difficult. Some are calling to abolish databases containing the identities of hundreds of thousands of people believed to be affiliated with gangs. Claims that gang data are invalid and unreliable only embolden critics.

However, eliminating gang databases could make it even more difficult to understand and respond to violence in communities.

The Current State of Gang Databases

In 2017, the city of Portland purged their gang database and halted the further collection of data on individual gang members. Other cities, from California to Illinois to New York, are facing calls to follow suit.

Law enforcement agencies throughout the United States maintain databases on gangs and gang members. At least 12 states have passed legislation pertaining to the development and use of gang databases, including how data should be gathered, stored and shared.

In 2012, the Department of Justice ended funding for the only validated national data source on gang activity, the National Youth Gang Survey.

Between the pullout of federal support for gang data and the growing movement to eliminate state- and city-level data, researchers and law enforcement now have less data on gangs. That makes it difficult to fact-check politicians who claim gang violence is rising, and who want to advance harsh immigration and crime control policies.

What Are Gang Databases Used For?

Gang data is important public safety information.

Far more Americans die at the hands of gang members than in acts of terror or mass shootings. Gang members account for a disproportionate share of crime and violence.

There are around 2,000 gang-related homicides every year, or 13 percent of all homicides in the U.S. The gang-related homicide rate alone in the U.S. (about 2 per 100,000 persons) exceeds the total homicide rate in nearly every European Union country.

In New York City, police report that 50 percent of all shootings in 2017 involved a gang member as either perpetrator or victim.

Amid a rise in gang violence in the mid 1980s, police began collecting data on gang members. Computerized gang databases were commonplace in large cities by the early 2000s.

Today, gang databases contain information on individuals and groups. Individual details include a person's name and other identifying information (e.g., tattoos), known associates, vehicles used or places frequented and criminal history. Group details include the evolution of gang symbols, the location of gang turf, and a gang's alliances and rivalries.

These data help the police solve gang-related crimes and flag gang members who might benefit from social services. They even help identify individuals who might leave gang life, if given the right nudge, such as an offer of employment.

In Boston and Cincinnati, a strategy to reduce violence called "Focused Deterrence" relies on such data to audit the gang landscape of cities and target offenders with deterrence messaging, which in turn has been shown to significantly reduce violence.

What's Wrong with Gang Databases?

There are four main arguments against gang databases.

First, opponents of data-gathering say that gang membership is not measured accurately. Social media and hanging out with gang members can create guilt by association. As activist Tamar Manasseh has argued, to the police, any black kid is in a gang.

Because of this, police overcount gang members. For example, a 2016 audit of California's gang database, CalGang, infamously revealed that babies and ex-gang members were listed as active gang members.

Second, people of color—particularly blacks and Latinos—are overrepresented in gang lists and this gives the perception of discrimination. Racial disparities were the primary driver behind the abolition of Portland, Oregon's gang database. In New York, less than 1 percent of the 17,441 people in the gang database were white. Critics say these numbers reflect an entrenched policing philosophy that has always criminalized the most vulnerable and marginalized people.

Third, gang databases are often kept secret, and as a consequence, there are potential due process problems. People listed in gang databases are rarely made aware of the designation and have little to no recourse to challenge it.

Finally, the consequences of being named in a gang database can be serious. Police stops involving "flagged" gang members are tense, and scrutiny can far outlast actual affiliation with a gang. In an era of data-driven policing, these concerns are important. Critics also point to the potential loss of employment and public housing, as well as criminal convictions and sentencing enhancements. In Chicago, one young man was inappropriately entered into a database for "loitering" in a neighborhood with high gang activity. He was living in the U.S. illegally and wound up in deportation proceedings.

What Does the Scientific Evidence Say?

There is merit to all of these criticisms, but a review of the evidence shows the issues are more complex. For example, a study found that twice as many juveniles report that they are gang members than are recorded in police records. The police are likely undercounting gang members just like they undercount crime, not overcounting.

The overrepresentation of people of color in gang databases is not solely an artifact of how the police collect information. Studies show that when people self-report that they are gang members, blacks and Latinos are twice as likely as whites to be gang members in adolescence and three to four times more likely in adulthood. Since gang databases like the NYPD's are overwhelmingly populated with adults, the research indicates that racial and ethnic disparities should be expected.

Police data on gang homicides fluctuate yearly with newspaper articles on gang violence and are reported consistently, especially in agencies with specialized police gang units. There is also high, but not perfect, correspondence between self-reports of gang membership and the names found in gang databases.

Finally, the criteria for inclusion in gang databases have been approved by the courts.

Keep the Baby, Drain the Bathwater

Eliminating gang databases altogether risks leaving law enforcement hamstrung in their efforts to reduce violence in communities. The opposite of bad data is not no data, but good data.

In the 1980s and 1990s, gangs proliferated outside of the urban core of U.S. cities. At the same time, officials denied their existence. For example, it took gang-related assaults on the mayor's son and governor's daughter in Columbus, Ohio, for that city to recognize its gang problems.

Improving data could be done with stricter, more consistent rules for who is a gang member and who isn't. The reports should undergo regular audits. Databases could also better reflect the fact that gang membership is a temporary status and even the "worst of the worst" are not beyond redemption.

States like California are showing how to improve information gathering on gang members. An audit of its database, CalGang, led Gov. Jerry Brown to sign legislation requiring law enforcement to notify individuals when they are entered into a gang database and allowing purported gang members the opportunity to challenge the designation.

If used correctly, gang databases can be part of the solution to violent crime.

VIEWPOINT 5

> "Online expression is central to democratic life, and various types of internet monitoring are known to suppress it."

Cookies Allow Government Entities and Corporations to Monitor Users
Elizabeth Stoycheff

In this viewpoint, Elizabeth Stoycheff explains how browser cookies are used to track user activity across websites and even devices, and how this tracking is used by both government entities and corporations. Most users do not pay attention to terms-of-service provisions on websites and consent to cookies without much thought. This is in part because the terms of service statements are designed to be frustrating with the intention of getting users to not put as much effort into rejecting cookies and avoiding online surveillance. Cookie notifications cause negative emotional reactions among users, which hinders access to information. Stoycheff asserts there should be changes to cookie designs going forward, but in the meantime, users should take the time to read websites' terms and conditions. Elizabeth Stoycheff is an associate professor of communication at Wayne State University.

"Browser cookies make people more cautious online, study finds," by Elizabeth Stoycheff, The Conversation, July 5, 2022, https://theconversation.com/browser-cookies-make-people-more-cautious-online-study-finds-184219. Licensed under CC BY-ND 4.0 International.

As you read, consider the following questions:

1. When were cookies developed, and what was their original purpose?
2. How is "friction" defined in this viewpoint?
3. What are examples of legislation regulating cookie notifications mentioned in this viewpoint?

Website cookies are online surveillance tools, and the commercial and government entities that use them would prefer people not read those notifications too closely. People who do read the notifications carefully will find that they have the option to say no to some or all cookies.

The problem is, without careful attention those notifications become an annoyance and a subtle reminder that your online activity can be tracked.

As a researcher who studies online surveillance, I've found that failing to read the notifications thoroughly can lead to negative emotions and affect what people do online.

How Cookies Work

Browser cookies are not new. They were developed in 1994 by a Netscape programmer in order to optimize browsing experiences by exchanging users' data with specific websites. These small text files allowed websites to remember your passwords for easier logins and keep items in your virtual shopping cart for later purchases.

But over the past three decades, cookies have evolved to track users across websites and devices. This is how items in your Amazon shopping cart on your phone can be used to tailor the ads you see on Hulu and Twitter on your laptop. One study found that 35 of 50 popular websites use website cookies illegally.

European regulations require websites to receive your permission before using cookies. You can avoid this type of third-party tracking with website cookies by carefully reading platforms' privacy policies and opting out of cookies, but people generally aren't doing that.

One study found that, on average, internet users spend just 13 seconds reading a website's terms of service statements before they consent to cookies and other outrageous terms, such as, as the study included, exchanging their first-born child for service on the platform.

These terms-of-service provisions are cumbersome and intended to create friction.

Friction is a technique used to slow down internet users, either to maintain governmental control or reduce customer service loads. Autocratic governments that want to maintain control via state surveillance without jeopardizing their public legitimacy frequently use this technique. Friction involves building frustrating experiences into website and app design so that users who are trying to avoid monitoring or censorship become so inconvenienced that they ultimately give up.

How Cookies Affect You

My newest research sought to understand how website cookie notifications are used in the U.S. to create friction and influence user behavior.

To do this research, I looked to the concept of mindless compliance, an idea made infamous by Yale psychologist Stanley Milgram. Milgram's experiments—now considered a radical breach of research ethics—asked participants to administer electric shocks to fellow study takers in order to test obedience to authority.

Milgram's research demonstrated that people often consent to a request by authority without first deliberating on whether it's the right thing to do. In a much more routine case, I suspected this is also what was happening with website cookies.

I conducted a large, nationally representative experiment that presented users with a boilerplate browser cookie pop-up message, similar to one you may have encountered on your way to read this article.

I evaluated whether the cookie message triggered an emotional response—either anger or fear, which are both expected responses to online friction. And then I assessed how these cookie notifications influenced internet users' willingness to express themselves online.

Online expression is central to democratic life, and various types of internet monitoring are known to suppress it.

The results showed that cookie notifications triggered strong feelings of anger and fear, suggesting that website cookies are no longer perceived as the helpful online tool they were designed to be. Instead, they are a hindrance to accessing information and making informed choices about one's privacy permissions.

And, as suspected, cookie notifications also reduced people's stated desire to express opinions, search for information and go against the status quo.

Cookie Solutions

Legislation regulating cookie notifications like the EU's General Data Protection Regulation and California Consumer Privacy Act were designed with the public in mind. But notification of online tracking is creating an unintentional boomerang effect.

There are three design choices that could help. First, making consent to cookies more mindful, so people are more aware of which data will be collected and how it will be used. This will involve changing the default of website cookies from opt-out to opt-in so that people who want to use cookies to improve their experience can voluntarily do so.

Second, cookie permissions change regularly, and what data is being requested and how it will be used should be front and center.

And third, U.S. internet users should possess the right to be forgotten, or the right to remove online information about themselves that is harmful or not used for its original intent, including the data collected by tracking cookies. This is a provision granted in the General Data Protection Regulation but does not extend to U.S. internet users.

In the meantime, I recommend that people read the terms and conditions of cookie use and accept only what's necessary.

Periodical and Internet Sources Bibliography

The following articles have been selected to supplement the diverse views presented in this chapter.

"Equity and Law Enforcement Data Collection, Use, and Transparency," Criminal Justice Statistics Interagency Working Group of the National Science and Technology Council, May 2023. https://www.whitehouse.gov/wp-content/uploads/2023/05/NSTC-Equity-and-Law-Enforcement-Data.pdf.

"Your Data Is Shared and Sold…What's Being Done About It?," Knowledge at Wharton, Wharton School of the University of Pennsylvania, October 28, 2019. https://knowledge.wharton.upenn.edu/article/data-shared-sold-whats-done.

Melissa Aronczyk and Maria Isabel Espinoza, "Who Benefits from Data for Good?," London School of Economics and Political Science, May 4, 2021. https://blogs.lse.ac.uk/impactofsocialsciences/2021/05/04/who-benefits-from-data-for-good.

Alton M. K. Chew and Dinesh Visva Gunasekeran, "Social Media Big Data: The Good, the Bad, and the Ugly (Un)truths," *Frontiers in Big Data*, June 1, 2021. https://www.frontiersin.org/articles/10.3389/fdata.2021.623794/full.

Arielle Pardes, "How Facebook and Other Sites Manipulate Your Privacy Choices," *Wired*, August 12, 2020. https://www.wired.com/story/facebook-social-media-privacy-dark-patterns.

Alex Reshanov, "How Bias Sneaks Inter Big-Data Policing," Life and Letters, The University of Texas at Austin, October 19, 2020. https://lifeandletters.la.utexas.edu/2020/10/how-bias-sneaks-into-big-data-policing.

Abdullah Shihipar, "Data for the Public Good," *New York Times*, October 24, 2019. https://www.nytimes.com/2019/10/24/opinion/data-privacy-research.html.

Zeynep Tufekci, "We Need to Take Back Our Privacy," *New York Times*, May 10, 2022. https://www.nytimes.com/2022/05/19/opinion/privacy-technology-data.html.

Nicol Turner Lee and Caitlin Chin-Rothmann, "Police Surveillance and Facial Recognition: Why Data Privacy Is Imperative for

Communities of Color," Brookings Institution, April 12, 2022. https://www.brookings.edu/articles/police-surveillance-and-facial-recognition-why-data-privacy-is-an-imperative-for-communities-of-color.

Justin Ye, "The Slippery Slope of Big Data in Policing," Harvard International Review, May 27, 2021. https://hir.harvard.edu/big-data-in-policing.

OPPOSING VIEWPOINTS® SERIES

CHAPTER 4

How Much of a Right to Privacy Should Internet Users Expect?

Chapter Preface

"Recent inventions and business methods call attention to the next step which must be taken for the protection of the person, and for securing to the individual . . . the right 'to be let alone.' " This plea for the right to privacy in the face of technological change sounds as though it could have been voiced by a contemporary internet user rights advocate. But it was written in 1890 by Louis Brandeis, the first American jurist to make the legal case for a right to privacy, even though it is not set out in the U.S. Constitution. Brandeis, who was concerned about privacy abuses presented by "instantaneous photography," could not have imagined the massive privacy threat now posed by data mining by governments and corporations.

The United States' internet restrictions are notoriously lax. But increasingly lawmakers are considering federal legislation to limit the personal information social media companies can collect from their users. In 2021, a Morning Consult poll found that 83 percent of Americans want Congress to pass a national data privacy act.

Internet privacy advocates also advocate for social media users to be allowed to remain anonymous. Many argue that people from marginalized groups might refrain from participating in internet discourse if they had to put themselves at risk by using their own names. Detractors, however, point to studies that suggest anonymity encourages at least some users to indulge in harsh, hateful, or even threatening language.

Another online privacy issue gaining traction is the "right to be forgotten." The European Union allows internet users to request that search engines stop linking to past comments or posts that could damage their reputation. The EU's measure challenges the oft-cited dictum "the internet is forever" by countering that users have a right, to the best of their ability, to make some online content temporary.

Digital Rights and Privacy

The set of viewpoints in this chapter address the controversy of whether data privacy legislation is needed, the debate over the utility of allowing internet users to remain anonymous, and the question of whether a "right to be forgotten" can or should be recognized and defended.

VIEWPOINT 1

> "U.S. citizens [are left] with minimal data privacy protections compared with citizens of other nations."

Internet Users Need More Rigorous Laws to Protect Their Privacy

Anne Toomey McKenna

In this viewpoint, Anne Toomey McKenna evaluates the present state of data privacy laws in the United States, which leave American internet users far more vulnerable to exploitation and abuse than users in many other nations with more stringent digital privacy regulation. She endorses the American Data and Privacy Protection Act (ADPPA), a proposed federal law that would override the piecemeal privacy protections enacted in some states, most notably California. McKenna particularly endorses a provision in the bill which allows consumers to sue tech companies for ADPPA violations. Anne Toomey McKenna is a visiting professor at the University of Richmond Law School, where she teaches international privacy law.

"A new US data privacy bill aims to give you more control over information collected about you – and make businesses change how they handle data," by Anne Toomey McKenna, The Conversation, August 23, 2022. https://theconversation.com/a-new-us-data-privacy-bill-aims-to-give-you-more-control-over-information-collected-about-you-and-make-businesses-change-how-they-handle-data-188279. Licensed under CC-BY-ND 4.0 International.

As you read, consider the following questions:

1. What is the American Data and Privacy Protection Act (ADPPA)?
2. What rights would the ADPPA grant to internet users?
3. Why do technology companies oppose the ADPPA?

Data privacy in the U.S. is, in many ways, a legal void. While there are limited protections for health and financial data, the cradle of the world's largest tech companies, like Apple, Amazon, Google, and Meta (Facebook), lacks any comprehensive federal data privacy law. This leaves U.S. citizens with minimal data privacy protections compared with citizens of other nations. But that may be about to change.

With rare bipartisan support, the American Data and Privacy Protection Act moved out of the U.S. House of Representatives Committee on Energy and Commerce by a vote of 53–2 on July 20, 2022. The bill still needs to pass the full House and the Senate, and negotiations are ongoing. Given the Biden administration's responsible data practices strategy, White House support is likely if a version of the bill passes.

As a legal scholar and attorney who studies and practices technology and data privacy law, I've been closely following the act, known as ADPPA. If passed, it will fundamentally alter U.S. data privacy law.

ADPPA fills the data privacy void, builds in federal preemption over some state data privacy laws, allows individuals to file suit over violations and substantially changes data privacy law enforcement. Like all big changes, ADPPA is getting mixed reviews from media, scholars and businesses. But many see the bill as a triumph for U.S. data privacy that provides a needed national standard for data practices.

International Privacy Laws

Facebook CEO Mark Zuckerberg's Congressional testimony will discuss ways to keep people's online data private, which I'm interested in as a privacy scholar. Facebook and other U.S. companies already follow more comprehensive privacy laws in other countries. But without comparable requirements at home, there's little reason for them to protect U.S. consumers the same way.

Inform Customers and Secure Data

U.S. privacy laws are mostly based on the Federal Trade Commission's Fair Information Practice Principles, which recommend companies:

- tell customers their data practices,
- give people some choice about additional uses,
- provide people with access to information about them, and
- ensure the security of the data collected.

In some industries, there are regulations for handling what's called "personally identifiable information." Federal laws protect medical information, financial data and education-related records.

Online services and apps are barely regulated, though they must protect children, limit unsolicited email marketing and tell the public what they do with data they collect.

Online tracking and advertising is self-regulated: Industry associations set rules for their members. Data collection by emerging technologies, such as smart speakers or self-driving cars, is mostly unregulated. The FTC does investigate if companies are "unfair or deceptive," but firms that prominently disclose what they do may avoid trouble.

Strong Limits on Data Collection

Europe, by contrast, generally prohibits collecting and using personal data. Its General Data Protection Regulation, which takes effect on May 25, applies to all businesses and government agencies in European Union member countries—including U.S. companies offering services in Europe.

continued on next page

The GDPR gives six reasons for collecting personal data. But even then, any analysis must be closely related to the purpose for which the data was collected. For example, a fitness-tracking company couldn't sell users' exercise data to a health insurance company without additional consent. Companies that violate the GDPR may be fined up to 20 million euros, or 4 percent of the firm's worldwide annual revenue.

Building on the GDPR, Europe's forthcoming ePrivacy Regulation will likely require explicit individual consent before a company can track a person's online activity.

Many other countries, including Mexico, Switzerland and Russia, have adopted comprehensive privacy regulations like the EU's. Canada also broadly regulates how government agencies and private companies use data.

The advantage of comprehensive privacy protections is that they're consistent across services and industries, even as new technologies emerge.

"Fragmented US privacy rules leave large data loopholes for Facebook and others," by Florian Schaub, The Conversation, April 10, 2018. https://theconversation.com/fragmented-us-privacy-rules-leave-large-data-loopholes-for-facebook-and-others-94606. Licensed under CC-BY-ND 4.0 International.

Who and What Will ADPPA Regulate?

ADPPA would apply to "covered" entities, meaning any entity collecting, processing or transferring covered data, including nonprofits and sole proprietors. It also regulates cellphone and internet providers and other common carriers, with potentially concerning changes to federal communications regulation. It does not apply to government entities.

ADPPA defines "covered" data as any information or device that identifies or can be reasonably linked to a person. It also protects biometric data, genetic data and geolocation information.

The bill excludes three big data categories: deidentified data, employee data and publicly available information. That last category includes social media accounts with privacy settings open to public viewing. While research has repeatedly shown deidentified data can be easily reidentified, the ADPPA attempts to address that by requiring covered entities to take "reasonable technical, administrative, and physical measures to ensure that the information cannot, at any point, be used to re-identify any individual or device."

How ADPPA Protects Your Data

The act would require data collection to be as minimal as possible. The bill allows covered entities to collect, use or share an individual's data only when reasonably necessary and proportionate to a product or service the person requests or to respond to a communication the person initiates. It allows collection for authentication, security incidents, prevention of illegal activities or serious harm to persons, and compliance with legal obligations.

People would gain rights to access and have some control over their data. ADPPA gives users the right to correct inaccuracies and potentially delete their data held by covered entities.

The bill permits data collection as part of research for public good. It allows data collection for peer-reviewed research or research done in the public interest—for example, testing whether a website is unlawfully discriminating. This is important for researchers who might otherwise run afoul of site terms or hacking laws.

The ADPPA also has a provision that tackles the service-conditioned-on-consent problem—those annoying "I Agree" boxes that force people to accept a jumble of legal terms. When you click one of those boxes, you contractually waive your privacy rights as a condition to simply use a service, visit a website or buy a product. The bill will prevent covered entities from using contract law to get around the bill's protections.

Looking to Federal Electronic Surveillance Law for Guidance

The U.S.'s Electronic Communications Privacy Act can provide federal law makers guidance in finalizing ADPPA. Like the ADPPA, the 1986 ECPA legislation involved a massive overhaul of U.S. electronic privacy law to address adverse effects to individual privacy and civil liberties posed by advancing surveillance and communication technologies. Once again, advances in surveillance and data technologies, such as artificial intelligence, are significantly affecting citizens' rights.

ECPA, still in effect today, provides a baseline national standard for electronic surveillance protections. ECPA protects communications from interception unless one party to the communication consents. But ECPA does not preempt states from passing more protective laws, so states can choose to provide greater privacy rights. The end result: Roughly a quarter of U.S. states require consent of all parties to intercept a communication, thus providing their citizens increased privacy rights.

ECPA's federal/state balance has worked for decades now, and ECPA has not overwhelmed the courts or destroyed commerce.

National Preemption

As drafted, ADPPA preempts some state data privacy legislation. This affects California's Consumer Privacy Act, although it does not preempt the Illinois Biometric Information Privacy Act or state laws specifically regulating facial recognition technology. The preemption provisions, however, are in flux as members of the House continue to negotiate the bill.

ADPPA's national standards provide uniform compliance requirements, serving economic efficiency; but its preemption of most state laws has some scholars concerned, and California opposes its passage.

If preemption stands, any final version of the ADPPA will be the law of the land, limiting states from more firmly protecting their citizens' data privacy.

Private Right of Action and Enforcement

ADDPA provides for a private right of action, allowing people to sue covered entities who violate their rights under ADPPA. That gives the bill's enforcement mechanisms a big boost, although it has significant restrictions.

The U.S. Chamber of Commerce and the tech industry oppose a private right of action, preferring ADPPA enforcement be restricted to the Federal Trade Commission. But the FTC has far less staff and far fewer resources than U.S. trial attorneys do.

ECPA, for comparison, has a private right of action. It has not overwhelmed courts or businesses, and entities likely comply with ECPA to avoid civil litigation. Plus, courts have honed ECPA's terms, providing clear precedent and understandable compliance guidelines.

How Big Are the Changes?

The changes to U.S. data privacy law are big, but ADPPA affords much-needed security and data protections to U.S. citizens, and I believe that it is workable with tweaks.

Given how the internet works, data routinely flows across international borders, so many U.S. companies have already built compliance with other nations' laws into their systems. This includes the E.U.'s General Data Protection Regulation—a law similar to the ADPPA. Facebook, for example, provides E.U. citizens with GDPR's protections, but it does not give U.S. citizens those protections, because it is not required to do so.

Congress has done little with data privacy, but ADPPA is poised to change that.

VIEWPOINT 2

> "We are privileging privacy in a way that sometimes can be harmful to the exact communities that we're trying to advance and protect."

Privacy Concerns Should Not Inhibit the Embrace of Useful New Technologies

Orly Lobel and Raju Narisetti

In this interview with journalist Raju Narisetti, author and law professor Orly Lobel cautions technology critics not to adopt an overly pessimistic view that leads them to accept positions that threaten the creation and implementation of new technologies that can help humankind, particularly vulnerable populations in the developing world. While addressing real concerns about digital surveillance and online privacy, she argues that some restrictions on technology can do more harm than good. For instance, she holds that a lack of useful data collection can hurt people more than over-collection, if the collected data can be used to improve human well-being. Raju Narisetti is the global publishing director for McKinsey & Company, and Orly Lobel is a law professor at the University of San Diego.

As you read, consider the following questions:

1. How have popular views of technology changed in the last several decades?

"Author Talks: In defense of big data," by Orly Lobel and Raju Narisetti, McKinsey & Company, November 7, 2022. Reprinted by permission.

How Much of a Right to Privacy Should Internet Users Expect?

2. What trade-offs should people consider when evaluating new technologies?
3. What does Lobel mean when she calls emerging technology "an equality machine"?

Public discourse is often wary of automation, AI, and data collection, but along with the risks of digital technology comes its power to address climate change and prevent discrimination.

In this edition of *Author Talks*, McKinsey Global Publishing's Raju Narisetti chats with Orly Lobel, a tech policy scholar and distinguished law professor at the University of San Diego, about her new book, *The Equality Machine: Harnessing Digital Technology for a Brighter, More Inclusive Future* (PublicAffairs, October 2022). Instead of trying to curb technological development—which Lobel says is not stopping any time soon—we can steer it toward a more equitable future. An edited version of the conversation follows.

What is the meaning of the book's title?

I wrote *The Equality Machine* and called it *The Equality Machine* to shift our mindset away from all of the bad, scary things that we are hearing about technology.

There is some truth—and sometimes a lot of truth—to the idea that algorithms, artificial intelligence, and digital technology can do harm, but I found that it's important to have a more nuanced conversation, where we can start thinking about what it would look like if we designed technology to be an equality machine, to be AI for good, to do the work that we need to do to have a fairer and more just society.

Why do you say tech has gone from being seen as generally good to generally evil?

We've had a shift over the past two decades. It's gone from a lot of excitement around new technology and an understanding that it can both have potential and problems, to having flat conversations about automating bias, automating inequality and surveillance, and having less and less privacy.

A lot of this has to do with alarmist misinformation about the direction that technology has been taking. Some of it has been about who has skin in the game in designing our technology systems. Justifiably, there is a concern about the concentration of who has the power to decide and design our digital systems. There's far too much concentration with big tech.

I have been involved in antitrust policy with the current administration and internationally. A lot of the fear of tech has to do with behavioral failures that we have. We as humans have an aversion to things that are less understood, less known. We have a psychological aversion to change. This has come together for a misinformed, flat, alarmist discussion about technology.

Given some of the risks of technological progress, how do we move forward?

To move forward, we need to do both: we need to be critical, but we also need to be cautiously constructive and optimistic. If we want to see progress, it's not enough to just say, "Let's ban algorithmic decision making. Let's ban biometric data collection."

What we need to do is ask questions and be sincere about what our goals are and what the trade-offs are between different choices that we are making as a society. This is the history of all human progress: there are always costs and benefits. There are risks, and we need to be asking what the failures have been, what the harms have been, and what the risks are, while also discovering best practices and discovering the potential.

I wrote *The Equality Machine* because in my research I find so many things to celebrate, so many great developments, and so many heroes, like computer scientists that are revolutionizing healthcare, health screening, and medical devices. There are also people making sure that we can detect salary gaps in the workforce and every other sector of life.

Part of the motivation of writing *The Equality Machine* is to show that in every field of life and in every sector that we care about, we have promising developments. So we need to know what the worst practices are, but we also need to have a vision and blueprint of the best practices.

Why isn't there a consensus on how to police technology?

The policy solutions on the table are quite limited right now. First of all, we are privileging privacy in a way that sometimes can be harmful to the exact communities that we're trying to advance and protect, and which can have more resources allocated to them. There is definitely a digital divide in the world.

What I show in the book is that we should be equally worried about not collecting data as we can sometimes be about collecting too much data and intruding too much on people's personal information.

We should absolutely be worried when data is not collected and when we leave some communities in different areas in the world—especially in the developing world—without access to digital data collection. We shouldn't have these [digital] divides between countries. We should understand that there are winners and losers from overprotection, just as much as there are winners and losers from underprotection of digital collection.

The conversations that we're having are divisive, and as a consequence, we aren't looking at constructive solutions that are robust, that involve collective action, and that involve investment in technology and experimentation.

There's a binary right now of either "private industry will take care of everything" or "private industry is the source of all evil," or "we need to focus on breaking up big tech and creating bans on technologies like facial recognition" or "we need to erect more walls on digital data collection."

Those are conversations that we need to have, but we aren't having the conversations about our core democratic values, and we have always had internal tensions within them. We value privacy. We value equality, health, and safety. We value speech, access, education, growth, and innovation.

We need to acknowledge that, in each system and in each kind of the new advancement in technology, there are going to be some trade-offs, there are going to be some difficult decisions to make, and those are the decisions that we have to make as a society.

Those are the kinds of conversations that we have to have: When do we value accuracy at some expense to privacy, for example? We're not having these conversations because we think that everything is right and left, that it's ideological.

Why are you optimistic for a future full of equality machines?

Sometimes it's hard to see the arc of progress when we're living through history and through a lot of things that are concerning at the moment. There are a lot of wrongs in the world.

Here in the United States, even compared to a decade ago, women have less reproductive rights than they had. Certainly, that's not a reason for optimism. And yet, I use this term "at the arc of history," or "the arc of progress," because it's important to look at the huge leaps that have been made for equality, for women, for minorities, and for people with disabilities for inclusion and accessibility and through technological advancements.

I set out to research all these wonderful things that are happening in medicine, in biotechnology, in technology, and in the platforms that help tackle hiring gaps, salary gaps, and even the dating markets.

I'm cautiously optimistic. I'm always asking about the risks. It's only when we have skin in the game and a constructive stance on envisioning the best possible future that we can get a brighter future and an equality machine.

VIEWPOINT 3

> *"Posting anonymously can allow people to protect themselves—to openly discuss and deal with complex topics safely."*

Internet Users Have a Right to Anonymity
Harry T. Dyer

In this viewpoint, Harry T. Dyer explains how online anonymity—concealing one's identity in online forums by using a false name and not revealing personal details—should not be blamed for harmful and hateful language on the internet. He cites that many abusive internet users use their own names, unafraid to reveal themselves because, due to lax platform moderation, they believe others in the platform or comments section will come to their defense if challenged. Dyer also argues that anonymity is a useful tool for people in marginalized communities to communicate safely online. Harry T. Dyer is a lecturer in education at the University of East Anglia.

As you read, consider the following questions:

1. What is online anonymity?
2. How can posting anonymously protect internet users from abuse?

"Online abuse: banning anonymous social media accounts is not the answer," by Harry T. Dyer, The Conversation, October 20, 2021. https://theconversation.com/online-abuse-banning-anonymous-social-media-accounts-is-not-the-answer-170224. Licensed under CC-BY-ND 4.0 International.

3. How can platform design and moderation be used to prevent abusive language online?

In the wake of the tragic death of the member of parliament for Southend West, David Amess, fellow MPs have been talking about how to best protect both politicians and the public from abuse and harm. This has included a strong focus on enacting laws designed to halt online abuse, even though police have not linked Amess's killing to this issue directly.

There have been suggestions that such abuse can be attributed, at least in part, to online anonymity—that is, the fact many social media users set up their accounts using aliases, and without images that reveal who they are, in order to conceal their identity. Speaking on Sky News, Home Secretary Priti Patel indicated there was a need to address anonymous accounts. Asked if she would consider legislation to remove the right to anonymity on social media, Patel responded:

> I want us to look at everything. And there is work taking place already […] But we can't carry on like this. I spend too much time actually with communities who have been under attack basically, who have had all sorts of postings put online, and it's a struggle to get those postings taken down. We want to make some big changes on that.

The idea has since gained traction, with other MPs calling for a ban on anonymous social media accounts as a way to mitigate online abuse.

Yet while it's clear there is a need to address how we engage with and on social media, removing anonymity isn't going to solve the problems of online abuse. In fact, removing the right to anonymity online could cause harm to many users, especially those from marginalised groups.

Anonymity as a Form of Protection

While there are many examples of people using anonymous social media accounts to abuse others online, it's equally clear that anonymity can be a lifeline to many users and communities. Posting anonymously can allow people to protect themselves—to openly discuss and deal with complex topics safely. It can allow people to speak out about abuse, and seek information.

For example, social media users in LGBTQIA+ communities have spoken about the importance of online anonymity as a way to negotiate discussions of sexuality safely, where disclosing their name might put them at significant risk of abuse and harm online and offline. Some said anonymity allowed them to access valuable information online as they navigated their own identities.

In my own research for my 2020 book about social media design and identity, my participants talked about the many ways in which they felt anonymity helped them to develop a sense of community. One participant discussed how social relationships were formed via comment boards with others using pseudonyms: "I know some really personal stuff about all of them, apart from the fact that I don't know their names."

While respondents did talk about incidents of abuse online from anonymous users, it was clear that equally, anonymity provided pathways to building communities and support networks. An insistence on real names can present barriers and challenges to already marginalised communities and users for whom "real names" are a complex issue. These include gender non-conforming users, drag queens, Native Americans and survivors of abuse.

Many Abusers Are Not Anonymous

Anonymity can be used to abuse "othered" groups such as women, LGBTQIA+ people and Muslims. However, research shows that people using their real names perpetrate abuse and bullying too.

On social media we continue to see users willing to say abusive things and share dangerous content with their full names, job titles and information on display. Banning anonymous social media profiles therefore isn't going to address the root of the hate we see online, be that directed at marginalised communities or at MPs.

Research shows Black and Asian female MPs face the most abuse aimed at female MPs online, suggesting the issue of anonymity is perhaps not the root cause of abuse, but a way for deeper social issues to manifest online. Katrin Tiidenberg and Emily van der Nagel write in their book *Sex and Social Media*:

> Whether anonymous or not, people look at existing posts and comments for cues regarding what is allowed in a particular online space and behave accordingly. It's not simply a matter of anonymous people being up to no good: platform design and moderation has a lot to do with what kinds of behaviours are allowed, and thrive, on social media.

I would agree with this, and call on platforms to take more responsibility for the communities they foster, and the voices and discourses they emphasise and minimise online. While it's refreshing to see politicians' desire to tackle online abuse, banning anonymity isn't the answer. Anonymity can be a vital lifeline for already marginalised communities, and removing it could inadvertently harm the very communities MPs seek to protect.

VIEWPOINT 4

> "Anonymity may make it easy for people to act antagonistically, unprofessionally, or unethically."

Anonymity Encourages Abusive and Hateful Speech in Digital Environments

Joe Dawson

This viewpoint by Joe Dawson employs a number of psychological studies to explore the connection between anonymity and toxic online behavior. While anonymity can encourage bad behavior in some internet users, it appears more potent when the dynamics of a group encountered online pushes individuals to use increasingly harsh language to impress and win the approval of other group members. The author also cites toxic social norms held by a group as another factor that might escalate harmful statements into cyberbullying and violent threats. The viewpoint notes that eye-contact might be a mitigating factor, leading to more cordiality even in anonymous digital settings. Joe Dawson is a digital communications specialist with the North Carolina Institute for Public Health.

As you read, consider the following questions:

1. How do group behavior and social cues encourage abusive language on the internet?
2. How can anonymity lead to cyberbullying?

"Who Is That? The Study of Anonymity and Behavior," by Joe Dawson, Association for Psychological Science, March 30, 2018. Reprinted by permission.

3. What positive aspects of online anonymity does the author cite?

In 1969, APS Fellow Philip Zimbardo of Stanford University dressed female students in lab coats, some plain with identity-concealing hoods, and some with name tags and no hoods. He told the students to give an electric shock to a confederate. The hooded participants were twice as likely to comply.

Zimbardo's study was a formative piece of a rich body of research showing a link between anonymity and abusive behavior. Scientists have found a tendency for many people to act rudely, aggressively, or illegally when their faces and names are hidden.

More recent studies, however, have identified the positive features of anonymity, including digital interactions that might be overlooked in the midst of the attention that "trolls" and hackers receive. Just like face-to-face gatherings in support groups like Alcoholics Anonymous, the Internet has offered people a chance to self-disclose and offer support without showing their faces or giving out their real names.

Behavioral studies on the role anonymity plays in online interactions have yielded mixed results. Overall, researchers have found that anonymity can reveal personality traits that face-to-face interactions may hide, but that it also allows strong group rules and values to guide individual behavior.

Group Coverage

In 1981, social psychologist Leon Mann demonstrated how being in a crowd can lead people to behave not only offensively, but violently. Mann studied newspapers from 1964 through 1979 to examine reports of apparent suicide attempts—specifically cases where someone threatened to jump off a tall building, bridge, or tower. Mann narrowed the reports to 21 instances that included crowds at the scene and found that in 10 of the cases, people encouraged the suicidal person to jump, and in three of the instances actually jeered when rescuers prevented the death. Mann found one instance in which the crowd screamed obscenities and threw stones and debris at the rescue squad. Factors such as the crowd's physical distance from the potential jumper (enabling their jeers to be heard but leaving faces impossible to identify) and the cover of darkness made the onlookers feel anonymous in ways that wouldn't arise in different types of crowd settings.

This phenomenon can also play out on crowded city streets and highways. Psychological scientist Patricia Ellison-Potter of the US National Highway Traffic Safety Administration, for example, has demonstrated in driving simulation experiments that people are more likely to drive aggressively when they are less visible (e.g., when driving in a car with tinted windows) than when they can be seen by other drivers (e.g., driving an open-top convertible).

Such group behavior is alive and well on the web. 4chan is often considered the putrid basement of the Internet, serving as a hub of racist, sexist, homophobic, grotesque images and text. 4chan's mostly anonymous users are known for trying to one-up each other, disgust and "troll" new users, and show that they have the lowest threshold for decency. They have conspired to harass the parents of a teen who killed himself and to flood epilepsy message boards with images that flashed suddenly and included patterns intended to induce seizures. While the site originally operated without moderation or any policing, 4chan site operators had step in to block child pornography from being distributed on the site.

A 2012 study from Marek Palasinski at the University of Lancaster in the United Kingdom tested males observing a mock chatroom that they were led to believe was real. The men were less likely to intervene after seeing an "older male" ask a "minor female" for personal details and nude photographs when a chatroom was composed of strangers rather than acquaintances, and in a room with many other users rather than just a few.

In a revealing 2001 study, Dutch social psychologist Tom Postmes and colleagues found support for the idea that behavior is shaped by the social identity of the group. Groups were asked to brainstorm solutions for a hospital having trouble meeting the needs of patients. Some anonymous groups were unknowingly primed with efficiency ideas, and they came up with efficient solutions for the hospital. When primed with friendly, positive, and helpful ideas, other groups came up with patient-oriented solutions. When the groups were not anonymous, this priming effect disappeared. Turns out, the room you're in can matter a lot.

In 2016, Postmes joined a team of psychological scientists, including APS Fellow Russell Spears (University of Groningen), in writing a short letter on the topic of anonymous groups for the journal *Behavioral and Brain Sciences*. In their conclusion, they wrote, "a rounded survey of the evidence shows that the problems of 'bad' groups do not lie in a generic "bad" group psychology but rather in specific "bad" group norms. Violent groups normatively validate violent action. Conformist groups normatively invalidate critical comment."

These authors also offer a prescription: "The solution to problematic behavior of crowds and groups is to challenge and change toxic group norms." Fixing the problem of online aggression, then, may be a matter of figuring out how to mold the norms of a given environment.

Anonymity and Social Cues

In a 2011 *Perspectives on Psychological Science* article, Jacob Hirsch, APS Fellow Adam Galinsky, and Chen-Bo Zhong write that people in anonymous settings tend to act on their natural disposition. Everyone can feel a sense of anonymity in a crowd, they say, but research suggests the aggressive individuals are the ones most likely to escalate violence.

Similarly, among Finnish spectators surveyed at a hockey game in 1997, individuals who self-reported that they would be more likely to break up a fight in the stands had lower measures of personality aggression than those who report they would not intervene.

Social cues, however, may also shape an anonymous person's behavior. In 2016, psychological scientists Adam Zimmerman of Florida International University and Gabriel Ybarra of the University of North Florida studied aggression in players of an unwinnable game. "Social modeling" was shown to have a large effect on their behavior. Anonymous participants responded more aggressively when they witnessed examples of aggression, and less so when they did not.

One-on-One

It doesn't take the protection of a group to unleash the nasty nature of anonymity. A 2016 study led by Christopher Bartlett of Gettysburg College surveyed college students and found that over the course of an academic year, people who felt that their identity was concealed online were more likely to report engaging in cyberbullying behavior and holding positive attitudes toward cyberbullying (e.g. "It's okay if someone deserves it.").

In Zimmerman's aforementioned 2016 study of player aggression, participants wrote about their experience playing the unwinnable game, and those with anonymous partners wrote more aggressively about those partners and rated themselves as being more tempted to humiliate or slap their partners on a survey compared to non-anonymous participants.

"It's very easy to take this shadowy image of this other person online and start using that to create this internal dialogue where you unleash all your stuff on this other person," says John Suler, a professor of clinical psychology at Rider University.

Suler, a pioneer in the field of cyberpsychology, published *The Psychology of Cyberspace*, a widely-used textbook on the psychology of the Internet, in 2001. He followed that book up in 2016 with *Psychology in the Digital Age*, which focuses on improving well-being in the context of our computer-centric lives.

When researchers have dug into the source of toxic behavior on the Internet, they have found it may not be anonymity itself, but the degree of obscurity, that influences an individual's conduct.

In 2012, psychological science researchers in Israel found that partners communicating by computer exhibited high rates of verbal aggression, what they called "flaming," in many anonymous or semianonymous conditions. When they were completely anonymous in a computer chat, when they used their real names, and when they could see each other's bodies from the side, verbal aggression was high, but not when a video put the two partners in eye contact. This suggests that eye contact may mark a major factor that separates aggression and cordiality—even when two strangers are locking eyes on screen.

Safe Sharing and Support

While anonymity may make it easy for people to act antagonistically, unprofessionally, or unethically, research has shown it can also make people unusually forthcoming and helpful. A 2010 study by University of Toronto researchers Vanessa Bohns and Zhong found that, in dark rooms versus bright ones, people were more likely to point out that strangers' pant zippers were undone or that they had food in their teeth, saving the strangers from possible embarrassment.

Sharing personal information and divulging secrets more frequently than in face-to-face communication is one of the most consistent findings of anonymity studies. Experiments and longitudinal studies in teens show that relationships started and maintained online are as stable and deep as relationships offline and that instant messaging and other communication technologies help people maintain relationships.

Clinical psychologist Sara Erreygers of the University of Antwerp in Belgium led a 2017 study looking at patterns of behavior in over 2,000 adolescents. She and her colleagues followed a cohort of 13-year-olds and found that being a cyberbully or being bullied doesn't reliably predict future bullying behavior, but positive behavior does have a "positive spiral" effect. Good deeds online beget future good deeds.

And this benign behavior isn't limited to completely anonymous contexts. A study in Switzerland found that sharing and self-disclosure about self-harm, depression, death of a parent, bisexuality, and other sensitive topics were high on YouTube video blogs, where users are not face-to-face, but are visually identifiable and occasionally use their real names.

Suler finds some paradox in such findings.

"On one hand, you feel protected and safe because your identity is unknown to the other person," he says, "but then you want to reveal all sorts of intimate things about yourself."

This type of Internet behavior doesn't seem to depend on the same aspects of communication as toxic online behavior does. The same researchers who tested which aspects of computer communication cause rude behavior ran a similar study on benign ones. They found that eye contact, which was a key variable in determining "flaming" online, wasn't the lynchpin for disclosure and prosocial behavior.

References

Bareket-Bojmel, L., & Shahar, G. (2011). Emotional and interpersonal consequences of self-disclosure in a lived, online interaction. *Journal of Social and Clinical Psychology, 30*(7), 732-759. doi:10.1521/jscp.2011.30.7.732.

Barlett, C. P., Gentile, D. A., & Chew, C. (2016). Predicting cyberbullying from anonymity. *Psychology of Popular Media Culture, 5*(2), 171-180. doi:10.1037/ppm0000055.

Christopherson, K. M. (2007). The positive and negative implications of anonymity in internet social interactions: "On the internet, nobody knows you're a dog". *Computers in Human Behavior, 23*(6), 3038-3056. doi:10.1016/j.chb.2006.09.001.

Crystal Jiang, L., Bazarova, N. N., & Hancock, J. T. (2013). From perception to behavior: Disclosure reciprocity and the intensification of intimacy in computer-mediated communication.*Communication Research, 40*(1), 125-143. doi:10.1177/0093650211405313.

Ellison-Potter, P., Bell, P., Deffenbacher, J. (2006). The effects of trait driving anger, anonymity, and aggressive stimuli on aggressive driving behavior. *Journal of Applied Psychology, 31*.

Erreygers, S., Vandebosch, H., Vranjes, I., Baillien, E., & Witte, H. D. (2017). Positive or negative spirals of online behavior? Exploring reciprocal associations between being the actor and the recipient of prosocial and antisocial behavior online. *New Media & Society*. doi:10.1177/1461444817749518.

Hirsh, J. B., Galinsky, A. D., & Zhong, C. (2011). Drunk, powerful, and in the dark: How general processes of disinhibition produce both prosocial and antisocial behavior. *Perspectives on Psychological Science, 6*(5), 415-427. doi:10.1177/1745691611416992.

Jacobsen, C., Fosgaard, T. R., & Pascual-Ezama, D. (2017). Why do we lie? A practical guide to the dishonesty literature. *Journal of Economic Surveys.* doi:10.1111/joes.12204.

Jessup, L. M., Connolly, T., & Galegher, J. (1990). The effects of anonymity on GDSS group process with an idea-generating task. *MIS Quarterly, 14*(3), 313-321. doi:10.2307/248893.

Joinson, A. N. (2001). Self-disclosure in computer-mediated communication: The role of self-awareness and visual anonymity. *European Journal of Social Psychology, 31*(2), 177-192. doi:10.1002/ejsp.36.

Lapidot-Lefler, N., & Barak, A. (2012). *Effects of anonymity, invisibility, and lack of eye-contact on toxic online disinhibition.* doi:10.1016/j.chb.2011.10.014.

Misoch, S. (2015). *Stranger on the internet: Online self-disclosure and the role of visual anonymity.* doi.10.1016/j.chb.2015.02.027.

Palasinski, M. (2012). *The roles of monitoring and cyberbystanders in reducing sexual abuse. Computers in Human Behavior, 28*(6) 2014-2022. doi:/10.1016/j.chb.2012.05.020.

Piazza, J., & Bering, J. M. (2009). *Evolutionary cyber-psychology: Applying an evolutionary framework to internet behavior.* doi:10.1016/j.chb.2009.07.002.

Postmes, T., Spears, R., Sakhel, K., & de Groot, D. (2001). Social influence in computer-mediated communication: The effects of anonymity on group behavior. *Personality and Social Psychology Bulletin, 27*(10), 1243-1254. doi:10.1177/01461672012710001.

Reicher, S. D., Spears, R., Postmes, T., & Kende, A. (2016). Disputing deindividuation: Why negative group behaviours derive from group norms, not group immersion. *Behavioral and Brain Sciences, 39.* doi:10.1017/S0140525X15001491.

Russell, G. W., & Mustonen, A. (1998). *Peacemakers: Those who would intervene to quell a sports riot.* doi:10.1016/S0191-8869(97)00177-3.

Valkenburg, P. M., & Peter, J. (2009). Social consequences of the internet for adolescents: A decade of research. *Current Directions in Psychological Science, 18*(1), 1-5. doi:10.1111/j.1467-8721.2009.01595.x.

Zhong, C., Bohns, V. K., & Gino, F. (2010). Good lamps are the best police: Darkness increases dishonesty and self-interested behavior. *Psychological Science, 21*(3), 311-314. doi:10.1177/0956797609360754.

Zimmerman, A. G., & Ybarra, G. J. (2016). Online aggression: The influences of anonymity and social modeling. *Psychology of Popular Media Culture, 5*(2), 181-193. doi:10.1037/ppm0000038.

VIEWPOINT 5

| "A person's right to be forgotten can clash with a person's right to know."

Internet Users Have a "Right to Be Forgotten"
Geeta Pandey

This viewpoint, which was written by Geeta Pandey for the BBC, details Indian actor Ashutosh Kaushik's struggle to remove personal information about himself from the internet. After winning fame and accolades for appearing on two reality shows in his native country, Kaushik was publicly shunned when videos of him during a drunk driving incident appeared on internet sites. Kaushik invoked a "right to be forgotten" to an Indian court—a right already recognized by the European Union. Although internet activists are fighting for a broader recognition of this right, it is not yet acknowledged in U.S. law. Geeta Pandey is the women and social affairs editor for BBC Online, India.

As you read, consider the following questions:

1. What is the right to be forgotten?
2. How did videos of one incident of drunk driving affect Ashutosh Kaushik's life for years afterwards?
3. What obstacles do people face in trying to remove negative personal information from the internet?

"Ashutosh Kaushik: Indian actor fighting for the 'right to be forgotten,'" by Geeta Pandey, BBC, February 17, 2022. Reprinted by permission.

How long should you be punished for a mistake?

That's the crux of Indian actor and reality show celebrity Ashutosh Kaushik's petition that the Delhi high court is due to hear on Thursday.

The actor wants the court to grant him the "right to be forgotten," stating that his life is still being held hostage to a mistake he "erroneously committed more than a decade ago."

Experts say the "right to be forgotten"—or the "right to erasure"—is simply the right to have your publicly available personal information removed from the internet. Although the right is recognised in the European Union—where it's not absolute—it's a fairly new concept in India and still not covered by law.

Kaushik hit the headlines when he won the fifth season of reality show MTV *Roadies* in 2007 and *Bigg Boss*—the wildly popular Indian version of *Big Brother*—a year later.

The wins, he says, earned him "accolades, love and appreciation of people from across India."

But fame gave way to infamy when, a year later, he was caught drink-driving.

A court ordered him to pay a fine of 2,500 rupees ($33; $25) and his driving licence was suspended for a year. He was also ordered to remain in court until the end of the day.

The incident made headlines because he was a celebrity. News reports, photographs and videos of what happened still populate the web and anyone searching for the actor can find them.

This, he says, has cost him dear—both personally and professionally.

"I was 27 then. I got everything I wanted so early in life. I'd lost my father and there was no-one to guide me. I was inexperienced and made a mistake and I was punished for it. But I'm 42 now, and I feel I'm still paying the price," Kaushik told me on the phone from Mumbai.

After the incident, he said, people started shunning him.

"Now the first impression people form of me is bad. I have lost out on work, I've been rejected for marriage several times, and every time I move home, my new neighbours look at me strangely."

His banker wife, Arpita, who married him in the summer of 2020, says her family has been prejudiced against her husband from the start because of the videos they saw on the internet.

"My relatives were very concerned about his past. My brother refused to accept our marriage and still doesn't talk to me. But I feel that everyone makes mistakes in life, so why should my husband be penalised for a lifetime?"

Kaushik adds, "When a court sentences an accused, it's for a 'term,' so the digital punishment should also have a time limit, a cut-off date."

Over the years, he says, he's approached several news websites and channels, requesting them to remove the articles, photos and videos, but most of them remain. He also wrote to India's information and broadcasting ministry and Google, but did not receive any response.

In his petition, the actor, who's done roles in Bollywood films such as *Zila Ghaziabad* and *Kismat Love Paisa Dilli*, says the articles cause him "deep agony" and "psychological pain." He wants the court to order the Indian government, the media watchdog Press Council of India and Google to "remove the content from various online platforms."

Kaushik is not the only Indian who's seeking the right to be forgotten. Dozens of similar petitions are being heard by courts across India—many of them from people who've been cleared of accusations against them or already served their sentences.

In one case, a woman in a matrimonial dispute wants a legal website to remove a trial court judgement from their site as it includes her address and other personal information.

The Indian government says its Personal Data Protection Bill, which is in the making, contains provisions related to the right to be forgotten.

A Google spokesperson told the BBC that their search "generally reflects what's on the web, so if people want content removed from the web, we ask that they start by contacting the independent sites hosting the content."

"Our goal has always been to support the greatest access to information possible . . . We work hard to provide systems that enable users to flag content that violates our policies, this includes removing unlawful content under applicable domestic laws," he added.

But technology expert Prasanto K Roy says at present there is no easy way for Indian citizens to exercise a right to be forgotten.

"The internet is a huge landscape with Google, the dominant gateway, and Microsoft's Bing. Then there's Wikipedia, Medium, all other intermediary platforms such as Facebook and Twitter, and tens of thousands of blogs."

Years ago, he says, he "spoke to Google informally for a woman who was repeatedly slandered and linked to 'husbands' she didn't have. But they weren't very helpful. In another case of a law enforcement officer whose name needed to be removed, informal requests didn't work but official channels did."

Google, he says, "can fairly easily block certain URLs or even search phrases which it does in the EU, mandated by law. But in India, the internet giant fears an explosion of such takedown demands, given how fragile and sensitive Indian social media is and how easily people take offence."

Lawyer Akshat Bajpai, who's representing Kaushik, says although there's a legal vacuum in India with regard to the right to be forgotten, there are court judgements which could be taken as precedents.

The high courts in Orissa and Karnataka have accepted the right to be forgotten as an essential part of the right to privacy. And in 2018, the Supreme Court said the right to privacy was a fundamental right.

"Fifty years later, when Kaushik's grandchildren google him, they would know he won the *Bigg Boss* and *Roadies*, but they would also know that he was involved in an unsavoury incident. He received the punishment he deserved under law, and now he has a right to privacy," Mr Bajpai says.

The issue, he adds, needs serious deliberation by the courts and society.

"A person's right to be forgotten can clash with a person's right to know. But I hope the court will find a middle ground—in heinous offences such as rape or murder, society has the right to know; but if the offence is not grave, perhaps the courts could allow the right to be forgotten."

> *"You may just have to accept that the world might not actually forget about the time when as a teenager your friend challenged you to shoplift."*

Individuals Cannot Expect to Erase All Embarrassing Online Information

Keith W. Ross

In this viewpoint, Keith W. Ross sets out to see how effective the European Union's right to be forgotten law was for removing personal information. In this account of his study, he explains that in most cases, by eliminating links on search engines to pieces of incriminating information, the law allowed people to hide personal details from friends and acquaintances. But he also discovered that, with enough computer skills and money, anyone could dredge up the "forgotten" information as well as discover who had made the request to remove the links to it. Keith W. Ross is a professor of computer science at NYU Abu Dhabi.

As you read, consider the following questions:

1. How can European Union residents make requests for information to be "forgotten" by the internet?

"Is anything ever 'forgotten' online?," by Keith W. Ross, The Conversation, July 11, 2016. https://theconversation.com/is-anything-ever-forgotten-online-61470. Licensed under CC-BY-ND 4.0 International.

2. How are internet users still able to obtain "forgotten" information?
3. What kind of information are most people requesting the "right to be forgotten" trying to hide?

When someone types your name into Google, suppose the first link points to a newspaper article about you going bankrupt 15 years ago, or to a YouTube video of you smoking cigarettes 20 years ago, or simply a webpage that includes personal information such as your current home address, your birth date, or your Social Security number. What can you do—besides cry?

Unlike those living in the United States, Europeans actually have some recourse. The European Union's "right to be forgotten" (RTBF) law allows EU residents to fill out an online form requesting that a search engine (such as Google) remove links that compromise their privacy or unjustly damage their reputation. A committee at the search company, primarily consisting of lawyers, will review your request, and then, if deemed appropriate, the site will no longer display those unwanted links when people search for your name.

But privacy efforts can backfire. A landmark example of this happened in 2003, when actress and singer Barbra Streisand sued a California couple who took aerial photographs of the entire length of the state's coastline, which included Streisand's Malibu estate. Streisand's suit argued that her privacy had been violated, and tried to get the photos removed from the couple's website so nobody could see them. But the lawsuit itself drew worldwide media attention; far more people saw the images of her home than would have through the couple's online archive.

In today's digital world, privacy is a regular topic of concern and controversy. If someone discovered the list of all the things people had asked to be "forgotten," they could shine a spotlight on that sensitive information. Our research explored whether that was possible, and how it might happen. Our research has shown that hidden news articles can be unmasked with some hacking savvy and a moderate amount of financial resources.

Keeping the Past in the Past

The RTBF law does not require websites to take down the actual web pages containing the unwanted information. Rather, just the search engine links to those pages are removed, and only from results from searches for specific terms.

In most circumstances, this is perfectly fine. If you shoplifted 20 years ago, and people you have met recently do not suspect you shoplifted, it is very unlikely they would discover—without the aid of a search engine—that you ever shoplifted by simply browsing online content. By removing the link from Google's results for searches of your name, your brief foray into shoplifting would be, for all intensive purposes, "forgotten."

This seems like a practical solution to a real problem that many people are facing today. Google has received requests to remove more than 1.5 million links from specific search results and has removed 43 percent of them.

'Hiding' in Plain Sight

But our recent research has shown that a transparency activist or private investigator, with modest hacking skills and financial resources, can find newspaper articles that have been removed from search results and identify the people who requested those removals. This data-driven attack has three steps.

First, the searcher targets a particular online newspaper, such as the Spanish newspaper *El Mundo*, and uses automated software tools to download articles that may be subject to delisting (such as articles about financial or sexual misconduct). Second, he again uses automated tools to get his computer to extract the names mentioned in the downloaded articles. Third, he runs a program to query google.es with each of those names, to see if the corresponding article is in the google.es search results or not. If not, then it is most certainly a RTBF delisted link, and the corresponding name is the person who requested the delisting.

As a proof of concept, we did exactly this for a subset of articles from *El Mundo*, a Madrid-based daily newspaper we chose in part because one of our team speaks Spanish. From the subset of downloaded articles, we discovered two that are being delisted by google.es, along with the names of the corresponding requesters.

Using a third-party botnet to send the queries to Google from many different locations, and with moderate financial resources ($5,000 to $10,000), we believe the effort could cover all candidate articles in all major European newspapers. We estimate that 30 to 40 percent of the RTBF delisted links in the media, along with their corresponding requesters, could be discovered in this manner.

Lifting the Veil

Armed with this information, the person could publish the requesters' names and the corresponding links on a new website, naming those who have things they want forgotten and what it is they hope people won't remember. Anyone seeking to find information on a new friend or business associate could visit this site—in addition to Google—and find out what, if anything, that person is trying to bury in the past. One such site already exists.

At present, European law only requires the links to be removed from country- or language-specific sites, such as google.fr and google.es. Visitors to google.com can still see everything. This is the source of a major European debate about whether the right to be forgotten should also require Google to remove links from searches on google.com. But because our approach does not involve using google.com, it would still work even if the laws were extended to cover google.com.

Should the Right to Be Forgotten Exist?

Even if delisted links to news stories can be discovered, and the identities of their requesters revealed, the RTBF law still serves a useful and important purpose for protecting personal privacy.

Digital Rights and Privacy

By some estimates, 95 percent of RTBF requests are not seeking to delist information that was in the news. Rather, people want to protect personal details such as their home address or sexual orientation, and even photos and videos that might compromise their privacy. These personal details typically appear in social media like Facebook or YouTube, or in profiling sites, such as profileengine.com. But finding these delisted links for social media is much more difficult because of the huge number of potentially relevant web pages to be investigated.

People should have the right to retain their privacy—particularly when it comes to things like home addresses or sexual orientation. But you may just have to accept that the world might not actually forget about the time when as a teenager your friend challenged you to shoplift.

Organizations to Contact

The editors have compiled the following list of organizations concerned with the issues debated in this book. The descriptions are derived from materials provided by the organizations. All have publications or information available for interested readers. The list was compiled on the date of publication of the present volume; the information provided here may change. Be aware that many organizations take several weeks or longer to respond to inquiries, so allow as much time as possible.

Ada Lovelace Institute

100 St. John Street
London, EC1M 4EH
United Kingdom
+44 (0)20 7631 0566
email: hello@adalovelaceinstitute.org
website: www.adalovelaceinstitute.org

The Ada Lovelace Institute is an independent research institute dedicated to ensuring that big data and artificial intelligence work for the benefit of people and society. Its aim is to prevent power asymmetries developing in AI.

Alan Turing Institute

British Library, 96 Euston Road
London, NW1 2DB
United Kingdom
+44 (0)20 3862 3352
www.turing.ac.uk

The Alan Turing Institute is committed to protecting society from the misuse and unintended consequences of AI and data technology. It is the national institute for data science of the United Kingdom.

Association for the Advancement of Artificial Intelligence (AAAI)

1101 Pennsylvania Ave., NW
Suite 300
Washington, DC 20004
(202) 360-4062
website: https://aaai.org

The AAAI is a scientific society devoted to advancing the scientific understanding of artificial intelligence. It also aims to improve the teaching and training of AI professionals.

Center for AI Safety

email: contact@safe.ai
website: www.safe.ai

The Center for AI Safety is a nonprofit using safety research, building the field of AI safety researchers, and advocacy to reduce the risks to society posed by AI. It identifies and addresses the potential dangers presented by AI.

Center for Human-Compatible Artificial Intelligence (CHAI)

2121 Berkeley Way, Office #8029
Berkeley, CA 94720
email: chai-admin@berkeley.edu
website: www.humancompatible.ai

The goal of the Center for Human-Compatible AI is to develop the technical ability to reorient AI research toward beneficial systems. It incorporates elements of the social sciences into its research to ensure that its benefits and impacts towards humankind are understood.

Future of Life Institute

933 Montgomery Ave. #1012
Narberth, PA 19072
email: contact@futureoflife.org
website: https://futureoflife.org

This non-profit organization is dedicated to guiding transformative technologies such as artificial intelligence away from risks and toward uses that will benefit life. It attempts to address potential risks through policy and outreach.

Human-Centered Artificial Intelligence (HAI)

Gates Computer Science Building
353 Jane Stanford Way
Stanford University
Stanford, CA 94305
email: hai-institute@stanford.edu
website: www.hai.stanford.edu

HAI is committed not only to promoting human-centered uses of AI, but to ensuring that the benefits to humanity from the technology are broadly shared. It is led by faculty from multiple departments at Stanford University.

Institute for Ethical AI & Machine Learning

website: https://ethical.institute

The Institute for Ethical AI & Machine Learning is a research center based in the UK. It develops frameworks to support the responsible development, deployment, and operation of machine learning systems.

Machine Intelligence Research Institute (MIRI)

548 Market Street
PMB 46597
San Francisco, CA, 94104
email: contact@intelligence.org
website: https://intelligence.org

MIRI is a research nonprofit whose mission is to develop formal tools that will make general AI systems safer and more reliable. It encourages AI developers to keep in mind the potential long-term impacts of the technology.

United Nations Environment Programme (UNEP)

United Nations Avenue
Gigiri Nairobi, Kenya
P.O. Box 30552, 00100
Nairobi, Kenya
+254 (0)20 762 1234
email: unep-executiveoffice@un.org
website: www.unep.org

UNEP is the world's leading authority on the global environment. The organization works to educate and enable people and nations to improve their quality of life and protect the environment for future generations.

Bibliography of Books

Philip Ball. *The Book of Minds: How to Understand Ourselves and Other Beings from Animals to AI to Aliens.* Chicago, IL: University of Chicago Press, 2023.

Susan Blackmore. *Consciousness: A Very Short Introduction.* Second Edition. Oxford, UK: Oxford University Press, 2017.

Meredith Broussard. *Artificial Unintelligence: How Computers Misunderstand the World.* Cambridge, MA: MIT Press, 2019.

David J. Chalmers. *Reality +: Virtual Worlds and the Problems of Philosophy.* New York, NY: W.W. Norton, 2022.

Brian Christian. *The Alignment Problem: Machine Learning and Human Values.* New York, NY: W.W. Norton, 2020.

Hannah Fry. *Hello World: Being Human in the Age of Algorithms.* New York, NY: W. W. Norton, 2018.

Sean Gerrish. *How Smart Machines Think.* Cambridge, MA: MIT Press, 2019.

Philip Goff. *Galileo's Error: Foundations for a New Science of Consciousness.* New York, NY: Pantheon, 2019.

Sam Harris. *Making Sense: Conversations on Consciousness, Morality, and the Future of Humanity.* New York, NY: HarperCollins, 2020.

Nicholas Humphrey. *Sentience: The Invention of Consciousness.* Cambridge, MA: MIT Press, 2023.

Gary Marcus and Ernest Davis. *Rebooting AI: Building Artificial Intelligence We Can Trust.* New York, NY: Pantheon, 2019.

Stuart Russell. *Human Compatible: Artificial Intelligence and the Problem of Control.* New York, NY: Penguin, 2019.

Anil Seth. *Being You: A New Science of Consciousness*. New York, NY: Dutton, 2021.

Janelle Shane. *You Look Like a Thing and I Love You: How Artificial Intelligence Works and Why It's Making the World a Weirder Place*. New York, NY: Little Brown, 2019.

Max Tegmark. *Life 3.0: Being Human in the Age of Artificial Intelligence*. New York, NY: Vintage: 2018.

Michael Wooldridge. *A Brief History of Artificial Intelligence: What It Is, Where We Are, and Where We Are Going*. New York, NY: Flatiron, 2021.

Index

A
ageism, 129, 136–138, 140
Alexa, 70, 75
Amazon, 26, 103
Anthropic, 20

B
bias, 15–16, 21, 94, 100, 102–103, 115, 118, 122, 129–156

C
Centre for AI Safety, 20–21
chatbots, 27, 44–48, 68–70, 75, 94, 115, 124, 131, 134, 154
ChatGPT, 14–15, 18, 20, 27, 45–47, 56–60, 67–69, 71–72, 94–96, 103, 115, 124, 131, 142
climate change and crisis, 18, 23–24, 34, 101, 124–125
Compas, 142, 143
consciousness, 15, 18, 56, 59–60, 62–66, 68, 70, 77–87, 92
Cortana, 70
customer service, 14–15
Cybertelecom, 32

D
Deep Blue, 58–59

deep learning, 45, 148
DeepMind, 20, 110
Department of Defense, U.S., 52

E
education, 40–41, 43, 120
ELIZA effect, 70
empathy, 73–76
environment, 23–27

F
Future of Life Initiative, 94–95, 111

G
Google, 20, 22, 26–27, 44–45, 47–48, 68, 95, 103, 110, 131, 134
government, 15, 32, 47, 76, 82, 97, 99–103, 107–113, 117–121, 124–125, 133, 137

H
health care, 18, 37–43, 76, 102, 120, 136–137, 148, 152–156

I

Institute for Ethics in AI, 21

L

large languages models (LLM), 14–15, 18, 56–58, 60–61, 63, 68, 71, 153–155

M

Meta, 21, 26, 103

Microsoft, 68, 72, 78, 94, 97, 103, 110, 131, 134

military, 52, 104–106, 123

misinformation, 15, 20–21, 30, 68, 94–95, 111, 115, 122–123

N

neural networks, 14, 44–45, 47, 50, 134, 148

O

OpenAI, 20, 22, 27, 72, 94–97, 99–101, 110, 122, 124

P

People-Centered Internet Coalition, 30

privacy, 96, 101–103, 109, 119

R

racism, 15–16, 119, 129–131, 133–134, 136–137, 143, 152, 154

robots and robotics, 32, 45, 71–72, 75, 81–87, 105, 144

S

sexism, 15, 129, 136–137

Siri, 70, 75

Stable Diffusion, 103, 115, 131

T

Turing test, 57–58, 69–70

U

UNESCO, 40–41

United Nations, 23–25, 27–28, 33

W

World Environment Situation Room (WESR), 24–25

World Health Organization (WHO), 38, 42, 137

This book is dedicated to all Hispanics who are committed to becoming new leaders.

"Reach perfection. No one is born that way. Perfect yourself daily, both personally and professionally, until you become a consummate being, rounding off your gifts and achieving eminence."

— Baltasar Gracian,
17th Century Spanish Jesuit priest